LIGHT FROM BEHIND THE BARS

Publisher's note

There are many who need to understand that the option of murder and violence as a means of redressing grievances or of changing the existing system or of achieving one's avowed purpose is not humanly acceptable in the community of peoples and nations.

There are others who are unable to forgive those who have brought death and destruction into their hearts and homes, offer them pardon and a chance to re-build their shattered lives. They live with a vengeance deep down in their beings which often brings them to the brink of desperation.

All these and many others – individuals, organizations and even States – need to "experience pardon and reconciliation, regaining for each the joy of hope". The publisher is proposing *Light from behind the bars* with the presumption that such "reconciliation and hope" is not only needed but possible and without it our world would be a sadder place to live in and our lives unbearable.

LIGHT FROM BEHIND THE BARS

Letters from the Red Brigades and other former Italian terrorists: true stories of terror, agony and hope

Edited by Carmelo Di Giovanni

 St Paul Publications

Original letters translated by William and Maria Laura Thuburn.
Revised and adapted by Simon Anholt

This book was first published in Italian under the title *Eravamo terroristi*,
Edizioni Paoline srl, Cinisello-Balsamo, Italy © St Paul Publictions UK

St Paul Publications
Middlegreen, Slough SL3 6BT, United Kingdom

Cover design: Mary Lou Winters fsp
Printed by The Guernsey Press Co., Guernsey C.I.

ISBN 085439 271 8

St Paul Publications is an activity of the priests and brothers
of the Society of St Paul who proclaim the Gospel through the
media of social communication

*This book is dedicated to
the yet unrepented and unreconciled*

Contents

A note
about terrorism in Italy

It's not easy to assign an exact date to the beginning of the twenty-odd years of terrorist activity which represent such a tragic period in recent Italian history. It is no less difficult to identify the causes behind this wave of violence, which escalated from sporadic guerilla encounters between rival left and right-wing groups, and culminated in all-out warfare, bombings and deaths.

The first bombing took place at the Banca dell'Agricoltura in Piazza Fontana, Milan, in 1969. Thereafter, the number of bombings gradually increased, and for a time there was almost one a year: one on a southbound express train at Gioia Tauro (Calabria) in 1970; one at Peteano Sicily) in 1972; another in Milan, this time in Via Fatebenefratelli, in 1973; one in Piazza della Loggia in Brescia and one on another train in 1974; and the bombers struck again with devastating effect at Bologna Station on 2nd August, 1980.

Many of these massacres went unpunished, and most recently, the supposed perpetrators of the Bologna Station episode have been cleared of any part in the crime.

Responsibility has been attributed to a series of groups and splinter groups, usually of the right wing. Possible links with the Italian secret services and various secret Masonic lodges are frequently talked about. From the admissions of a number of *pentiti* – the repentant, ex-terrorist collaborators – a part of the truth has emerged, but it is still only a fragment of the whole picture. Thus, in the course of this book, names and abbreviations of organizations appear and disappear, the products of splits between groups and subgroups. It's all a tactic, a game of hide-and-seek, and part of the instinct towards heightening the general state of confusion and tension.

In 1968 the number of works' action groups began to

increase – groups like *Potere Operaio*, or "Workers' Power", and *Lotta Continua*, "Continuous Struggle", and the first phase of real armed conflict dates from the disintegration of these movements. The massacre at Piazza Fontana was the first move towards the so-called *strategy of tension*, which aimed to create a general state of danger and alarm, so that an authoritarian, neo-Fascist regime, promising a return to order, could then be offered to a grateful public.

The "Armed Struggle" was simply the extreme Left's response to this scheme; and in November 1969, a strike of the metalworkers' union took a violent turn when an officer of the *carabinieri* was killed.

Many of the groups that were formed during this period failed to hold together, whilst others gained strength and purpose from the idea of avenging acts perpetrated by the other side, and the general tenor of these groups became ever more extremist, especially in cases like the riots at the Sit-Siemens and Pirelli factories. And thus the Red Brigades came into existence.

In 1974 the *Nuclei Armati Proletari*, or "Armed Proletarian Units" were formed in Naples, and they too became part of the movement. In 1977 *Prima Linea*, the "Front Line", was born, whose leaders went on to play active parts in the Red Brigades and in *Lotta Continua*. 1977 was a crucial date, when Luciano Lama, the secretary of the left-wing trade union organization CGIL, was hissed and shouted down by students occupying Rome University. This was the start of a wave of protest which quickly escalated into armed violence; the young protesters mounted a full-scale insurrection, organizing armed marches, looting shops, and charging police cordons. Shots were fired and lives lost on both sides. A movement called *Autonomia Operaia*, "Workers' Autonomy", was formed. *Lotta Continua* was disbanded and a group called *Senza Tregua*, or simply "No Truce", was formed from its ex-members; they went on to become the nucleus of the "Front Line" in 1976. *Prima Linea* is a well-known name in Italy, and the terrorist acts perpetrated by its members are among the most vividly remembered by the general public. Various other like-minded organizations, such as the *Comitati Comunisti Rivo-*

8

luzionari, (or *Co. Co. Ri.*), the Revolutionary Communist Committees, are equally notorious.

By 1975, the pattern was already set for ever-more violent confrontations between the left-wing "red" and right-wing "black" groups. Up until this point, the armed struggle had been a series of demonstrations – arson, knee-capping, kidnappings and so forth – but now the planned assassinations began: and there were many. The most brutal of these was the murder of Aldo Moro, the President of Italy's Council of Ministers (Prime Minister). This was an act which marked the penetration of the Red Brigades' activities into the heart of the State.

Moro was kidnapped on 16th March 1978, in a bloody attack during which his five-man escort was killed. After this event, there was a split within the armed faction; there were many arrests, and many of those arrested began to talk. The Red Brigades and *Prima Linea* were in turmoil.

But there were many more victims yet to come. Two "commandos" from *Prima Linea* killed Emilio Alessandrini, vice State Prosecutor in Milan, on 29th January 1979, and Guido Galli, the Examining Magistrate in Milan, on 19th March 1980. In 1980, a group known simply as "28th of March", which was mainly made up of students, murdered the *Corriere della Sera* journalist, Walter Tobagi. In the same year, the Vice-President of the Supreme Court of Magistrates, Vittorio Bachelet, one of Italy's highest judiciary authorities, was murdered at Rome University, where he lectured. In 1981, the American General, James Lee Dozier was kidnapped; he was later freed by the Italian equivalent of the British SAS.

Dozier's release and the arrest of his kidnappers came as a mortal blow to the Red Brigades, already weakened by the arrest and "repentance" of Patrizio Peci, one of their high-profile members. The Red Brigade terrorists wreaked their revenge by killing Peci's brother, Roberto; but the confessions continued. A large number of active cells were brought to light, and many more militants of the armed struggle were brought to justice.

In 1982, a law was passed allowing special leniency for repentant terrorists, and this proved a significant contribution to the fight against terrorism. Another important victory lay in the ever-increasing numbers of *dissociati* – the arrested terrorists who agreed to dissociate themselves from the principle of political violence and publicly renounce it, without however going to the extent of collaborating with the authorities and revealing names and places, as the *pentiti* did.

Yet there were further killings to come: the American diplomat Leamon Hunt in 1984; the professor of industrial economics Ezio Tarantelli; in 1987, General Giorgieri of the Italian Air Force; and on 18th April 1988, senator Ruffilli, political adviser to the Prime Minister, a murder which the terrorist Bruno Laronga discusses in this book.

But according to some experts on terrorism, of the dissolution of the movement was already in act in 1984, when the last two members of *Prima Linea* were arrested.

And this date marks the beginning of another phase in the history of the terrorist movements: the phase of their trials in court, and the dawning of a sense of responsibility amongst the perpetrators of violence, and their decision to admit responsibility for their actions and provide vital information about the strategies, places, and people involved. And so the principle of dissociation from the armed struggle was engendered.

It was during this period that the *Aree Omogenee di Dissociazione*, or United Dissociation Groups, began to be formed in various Italian prisons, and primarily at Rebibbia jail in Rome. These were associations of right and left-wing ex-terrorists who met in prison to discuss politics and human questions in a new atmosphere of peace, toleration and understanding. Both Livio Lai and Arrigo Cavallina talk at length about these groups in their sections of the book.

Introduction

As a magistrate in the Milan office of the State Prosecutor, I have been dealing with terrorism and political subversion since 1977. From September 1978 until mid-1985 this engaged me virtually full-time, whilst in more recent years as the phenomenon decreased, I began to take an interest in other matters, and especially those related to Mafia crime.

I am now forty two years old and was not yet thirty when I dealt with my first terrorist trials as a public prosecutor. And I was still relatively young when, in 1979 and 1980, I first witnessed the phenomenon of former terrorists opting for active dissociation. Cooperating with the authorities, they told us about the structure and the composition of the groups that had bathed Italy in blood; and thus they contributed to their eventual dissolution.

I then had direct experience of that second, more widespread form of political self-criticism (which was certainly encouraged by the first kind, but which, conversely, did not always result in proper collaboration with the State) which is usually referred to simply as "dissociation" – not active dissociation, in this case – from armed struggle.

I was a close friend and pupil of Emilio Alessandrini and Guido Galli, two colleagues in Milan killed by Prima Linea (The Front Line), a left- wing revolutionary movement, the former on 29th January 1979, and the latter on 19th March 1980. I had worked for a long time on terrorist trials with Galli in particular, and I admit I held him in some reverence both as a judge and as a man. I rushed to the scenes of both murders. On the day of Emilio's murder I was on duty elsewhere, but on 19th March 1980, I worked with Guido all morning until a few hours before his death.

I clearly remember the entry in Guido's diary, "If something should happen to me, call the magistrate Armando

Spataro", followed by my telephone numbers. I am an intimate friend and frequent visitor of my two colleagues' families and I have assisted one of Guido's daughters, Alessandra, in her professional training after her success in the State magistrature examinations. I also got to know their assassins very well, and since several of them have collaborated productively with the judiciary, I have petitioned for reductions in their sentences, as I have subsequently done for others. Several laws, in exceptional circumstances, allow for this.

I felt that this brief premise was useful as I believe it serves to explain why I was asked to write these introductory pages for Fr Carmelo Di Giovanni's book, and why I unhesitatingly agreed to do so. I believe it also serves to explain the thinking behind some of my views.

I was undoubtedly chosen because I was working in the field, because I was a magistrate who had acquired a profound knowledge, over a long period of time, of the phenomenon of terrorism; but also because I had played a leading role in these rather traumatic events. My role has been seen by some as somehow contradictory, since in my duties as public prosecutor I took on many occasions a stand of notable and rigorous firmness whilst in others I advocated, before the judges involved, the maximum leniency provided by law for the so-called "pentiti" – the repentant terrorists.

All that I have said so far, whilst of course it has no bearing upon my obvious and absolute respect for the laws enacted by Parliament, bears witness to a particular human experience of mine. It is clear that although my attitudes as a public prosecutor sometimes appeared contradictory, sometimes even in the case of the same defendant, they were essentially influenced by changes in that person who stood accused in front of me.

By this I mean that I have always seen even the arrested terrorist who has killed, and who may indeed have wanted to kill me, in his entirety as a human being with all his tensions, impulses, ambiguities; and that the laws which I applied and whose application I petitioned for in respect of a given terrorist, albeit necessarily abstract and inevitably imperfect, were nonetheless laws which left room for taking stock of the changes which every person can undergo. Firmness was, therefore, our response to the "hardness" of the terrorist and to his passion for destruction; and leniency was not the product of some supposed official hypocrisy. It was both a careful choice made by the State (which of course desired to oppose this subversive phenomenon and save human lives), and at the same time a very apt acknowledgment of the changes the person had undergone, and of the need always to mete out punishment in proportion to the real potential risk of that person.

This is also the story of people and their experiences, not simply a record of trials, legal formulas, statistics. Nor is it a story of blind repression, as some still maintain – even, oddly enough, some of those whose letters are published in this book. But I will return to that later.

And so to the book. This book is really the story of people who made mistakes, were arrested, and have changed, first within themselves, and then in their relationships with others. They are gradually re-building social relationships and in many cases experiencing new commitments. I want to talk briefly about them and of the humanity which emerges from their letters.

But I would first like to talk about Father Carmelo. During those long years in which I was involved with terrorism, I got to know many clergymen and religious women who worked with the convicted, and with many of the relatives of their victims too. They became leading figures in these dramatic events. The role of these people has been, in my opinion, of very great importance in making many ex-terrorists understand that desiring a more just society is irreconcilable with the politics of oppression; that tolerance does not mean renouncing one's own beliefs in the least; and that people's faith can be won day by day, step by step, even in the face of total scepticism.

I am thinking of people of Antonio Riboldi's calibre – the Bishop of Acerra – of Father Adolfo Bachelet – Jesuit priest, brother of the murdered judge Vittorio Bachelet; of the irrepressible Sister Teresilla; and there are others

13

whom I have certainly forgotten to mention. I knew them, I appreciated their worth, I helped them as much as I was able in their difficult mission, and I have also obtained real support and comfort from them when I have faced difficult moments in my own work.

Among the clergymen I have known and admired, however, Father Carmelo holds a special place; not, of course, because he deserves more or less credit than the others (such distinctions are meaningless in this field) but because his experience is unique and his personality remarkable.

I got to know Father Carmelo several years ago, through Mario Ferrandi, a prisoner sentenced in several trials which I had conducted, and who had reached a position of almost complete co-operation with the judiciary, after a process of notable personal suffering. Ferrandi had a background of quite high-level militancy, in various subversive groups and connected activities. But he had conceived a project which he worked at in an almost obsessive way, trying to involve all his ex-terrorist colleagues, even those who seemed to be quite insensible to certain kinds of thinking, in a general process of self-criticism. In this way he hoped to make their full social rehabilitation a real possibility.

I will not disguise the fact that at the time his efforts seemed impossibly utopian to me, and I am of course delighted that events have since proved me wrong.

I was surprised to learn, however, that Ferrandi, recently extradited from Great Britain (where he had been arrested) kept in close touch with a certain Father Carmelo, an Italian priest who visited British prisons to give help and moral support to Italians detained there.

In fact Ferrandi spoke to me about this Father Carmelo so enthusiastically and described his activities in such a vivid way that I could scarcely imagine how a man of the Church could be so dynamic, so active; how he could be involved in a hundred-and-one different projects, could be so likeable and so well-loved by the prisoners who had got to know him – and could have the power to awake in the most violent right-wing extremists a spirit of genuine self-criticism.

London in that period was, in fact, a place where numerous wanted people went to hide. Many have subsequently been arrested, the members or ex-members of revolutionary neo-Fascist groups. Ferrandi asked me if he could give my name to Father Carmelo, who could then contact me and obtain legal information of a technical nature, which would be useful to him in his work of re-educating prisoners.

Naturally I gave my permission and after a few letters or telephone calls, I met Father Carmelo in my office on the occasion of one of his visits to Italy. He was different from the way I had imagined him. I liked him immediately, and in the course of our subsequent meetings, I found I soon felt able to call him simply Carmelo, not Father.

I talked about him later with Ferrandi, I received more letters from him, and I wrote back to him. We spoke occasionally on the telephone. Certainly, I cannot say that I know him intimately but I feel I am a friend of his and I would like to go and see the actual places where he works.

I cannot exactly define what makes his enthusiasm so infectious and why I felt encouraged to trust him immediately (as I think everybody does who meets him). It may be something to do with his past as a "left-wing priest", which he himself describes so vividly in the opening pages of this book, or perhaps it is because he is almost literally bursting with the spiritual energy of a man who has travelled half the world and lived through some unique experiences. Perhaps it is to do with the complex story of how he came to be involved with prisoners, terrorists and ex-terrorists; or perhaps because a priest who works abroad does excite one's curiosity, especially in a situation as complex as I imagine the English one to be.

But I think his most remarkable characteristic is probably his way of doing things, his natural ability to put people at their ease when he talks to them, without daunting them with the gravity of the issues under discussion. This is the serenity of a man who has travelled a difficult road: but it is also his ability to be a priest and exercise his ministry whilst retaining the ability to see beyond all the common formulas and procedures, and yet without raising doubts or scepticism in others, or encouraging them to reject his approach.

I would like to have had more time to speak with Carmelo but I can see how he has become a crucial influence for many prisoners, and how the political militants in particular have opened their hearts to him, confiding in him their own anxiety, their continuing doubts, their maturer recognition of the mistakes they have made, the desire to be believed and accepted by society once again. They have done this because they have recognized in Carmelo a man who fully understood them, and who asked nothing in return for the friendship which he gave them, who has no vested interests or indeed any principles other than the purely ethical and moral.

And this is why it is such a magnificent idea to collect together the letters of people convicted of acts of terrorism: these are letters written by people in search of a real intermediary who has no official role, someone who wants to be their friend, who is prepared to listen to them and believe that they can change – can change in a way that Carmelo, like each one of us, has experienced too. I also, as a magistrate, have sensed and subsequently seen proof of such changes in many of those who stood accused in my courtroom: even I – fortunately – find myself changing as the years pass.

All in all, it seems to me that this collection will serve as a useful example to everybody. It will be useful to the writers of the letters, to help them understand that every failure brings its own prospect of regeneration, and that one's neighbour is not always the devil one imagines. It will enable those who read it to attempt to glance into the souls and minds of people who too often and too hastily have been labelled as monsters; and above all to understand that even monsters can change – and not invariably by means of plastic surgery.

But it would be dishonest of me not to admit that a careful reader can, in my opinion, tell from the different types of language used (and I am not talking here about how well or how badly the letters may have been written, but about their actual content) just how far the different writers have really progressed in their process of self-criticism. The careful reader can also single out those areas of ambiguity which still surface here and there in some of the letters. Let me put it another way. I am personally acquainted with several of the writers of the letters published in this book, and with many of them (I am thinking of Mario Ferrandi, Marco Barbone and one or two others) I would have no difficulty in having an ordinary social relationship, were it not for certain objective circumstances such as the age difference, and a certain sense of embarrassment which, despite everything, still prevails between people who have once confronted each other in roles as antagonistic as accused and Public Prosecutor.

But it often happens that I have a cup of coffee at the bar with these young people, or find myself chatting with them about any number of issues which have nothing at all to do with their past. What does this mean? That we have all simply expunged the past and the tragedies that they have caused? Or does it mean that I, as a magistrate, continue to regard them as repentant collaborators and that as such they deserve special treatment?

Nothing of the kind; it simply means that one citizen, who also happens to be a magistrate, is perfectly aware that in front of him stands a group of people who are different from the people he knew at the moment of their arrest. These are human beings who have changed, and who have won back the right to be considered as human beings, because the change they have suffered has been achieved by their own unambiguous recognition of their guilt and of the mistakes they have made. Is there any means by which they could adequately have compensated the victims of all those tragedies, even supposing they had had billions of Lire at their disposal? Of course not. But they could certainly compensate the society which they had attempted to destroy simply by offering their own contribution of truth.

Indeed it is obvious that as a society we will never feel confidence and certainty about our future unless we are unalarmed by the dramatic and mysterious dangers which make up our recent and more remote pasts.

So these young people have paid a tribute which is appreciable in human and civil as well as in religious terms, since, as Carmelo emphasizes in his introduction, they have understood that good and evil are present within each of us, and that it is quite, quite wrong for them to attribute the evil they have done to the evil in others, in order to shift the blame or arouse sympathy.

If all this is true, then I consider that continuing to insist that the responsibility for certain insensate actions is attributable to society in general, to the State, to its institutional system, to repressive policies which have been carried out by the judicial, penal and police authorities, is not merely anti-historical with regard to the times in which we live, but incompatible with our avowed aims of encouraging self-criticism, and disrespectful to social sensitivity and to the rights of the victims and their relatives.

No, I will not share this view; and I wish it to be quite clear that this is not because I believe this State to be perfect, or truly democratic, or that its institutions are immune from blame or free of all irregularity. But one must have the courage, and never abandon it, to say quite clearly, that nothing whatsoever can justify armed struggle in the way it has been carried out in this country (Italy) in the last two dramatic decades.

As it happens, the vast majority of the authors of the letters collected here (and I am referring above all to those eight or ten whom I know personally) got beyond this sort of deceit – or call it ambiguity, at the very least – some time ago.

But in some of the letters, assertions of the type which I have criticized earlier still come to the surface, albeit within the framework of that process of self-criticism which seems so unquestionably serious and hard-won. Frankly I prefer not to name names, and so must overcome my natural aversion to generalizations – which are almost always unjustified – since at this moment I am not acting in my institutional role as a public prosecutor. I do not have to petition the Court for sentences or pardons, lengthened or lightened; but as a man and a magistrate, I am expressing my judgement of the content of a book of great social significance. I hope, therefore, that certain ambiguities which now and again I believe I can detect are nothing more than the price that some have yet to pay before setting their conscience at peace again; that peace which is obtained from the knowledge of not having lied, and above all not to oneself. And I am certain that in this respect Carmelo's support will be decisive. His open and irresistible smile will encourage those who are uncertain; other books might follow this one, further evidence of a re-integration that really worked, of a forgiveness which is not the kind that can be sought and perhaps even won through politics, but the kind that is deserved and won through actions.

Armando Spataro
Deputy State Prosecutor in Milan

Carmelo recounts

For well I know my misdeeds.
And my sins confront me all the day.
Restore to me the joy of your salvation.
Then I will teach transgressors your ways.

Psalm 51

Why this book?

In the last 15 years, in my pastoral activity of visiting prisoners, I have got to know a great many people. From these contacts a living testimony has gradually emerged, fed by the thousands of letters exchanged with the prisoners and their families.

After years of silent work I realised that the message enclosed in these letters was of great value, too precious to stay hidden away in a drawer.

So I thought I would gather together the most significant letters written by drug addicts, terrorists, Aids sufferers and their families, which build up a dramatic picture of desperate men and women, their suffering and anguish in the face of the collapse of their lives, and of the pain caused to others. But in certain passages which at first seem tortuous and hopeless, a second picture emerges; and it is a message of hope and renewal.

When I spoke about this plan with some friends at St Paul Publications in London, they advised me to separate the experiences of the so-called political offenders from those of other prisoners. It was a suggestion which I rejected at first, not wanting to create "categories". Then I realised that we were in fact dealing with different experiences and different processes of enlightenment, and it was right to give each of them a different framework and emphasis.

So I accepted this idea of distinguishing between different cases, but not in order to adhere to a trend which is currently fashionable, nor to cause a sensation, nor to vindicate some kind of historical hypothesis, but because

I am convinced that the crucial message of these testimonies is this: God has through his love the power to alter – slowly and with much suffering – the hearts of men, even of terrorists. That makes these pages worth reading. The tragic experiences which they mirror can become in themselves a reason for conversion.

In conclusion I wish to thank everyone who has made this book possible; the writers of these letters who allowed me to publish them, and with them all those who asked me not to include theirs, preferring their spiritual experience to remain untold.

My thanks also to the Magistrate Armando Spataro for having accepted with enthusiasm to write such a fresh and sincere preface; Fr Roberto Russo, Parish Priest of the Italian Church at Clerkenwell, London, for his moral and material support, and especially William Thuburn and Maria Laura Franciosi, journalist with the Italian Press Agency, ANSA, whose assistance in the drafting of the book has been fundamental, and Simon Anholt for revising the English translation.

My first meeting with a "political prisoner"

The protagonists of this book are people who recognize the harm which they have done and seek purification through the love of God.

I had already been giving pastoral care to Italian prisoners in British prisons for some years, but I had never come across a "political prisoner".

One day, two Italians were arrested in London. They were from Milan and belonged to Prima Linea, "Front Line". I didn't even know that they were political militants. One of them was immediately released; the other was Mario Ferrandi.

Two things particularly struck me about him; his hatred for the "pentiti", or repentant terrorists, who had accused him in Italy; and the way he explained the motives which had led him into becoming a terrorist – his desire for a more just society, and for more social justice – aims which he believed could be achieved through violence.

22

I remember that I spent a lot of time simply listening to him, making few comments and passing few judgements. Only after months of such meetings (I went to see him continually) and after I had understood his way of thinking, did I begin to talk to him about God, Jesus Christ, and the Church, in the light of my own personal experience. In him I could clearly see myself as I had been in past years. I felt empathy with what he was saying. I remember that every so often, whilst he spoke, my old mentality would awaken. I understood him, I would agree with what he was saying: then I would have to stop myself, saying, "This is not the answer."

I tried to make him understand that nothing can be achieved through violence. "We'll just end up with a heap of rubble and corpses and we won't have resolved anything", I told him. And I began to explain Christ's mission as a Suffering Servant. "True revolution", I told him, "isn't marching down the street and throwing rocks at the police or your enemies, planting bombs and laying ambushes. Real revolution is taking up the burden of other people's errors."

"Christ", I said, "loved us when we were wicked. He defeated evil by accepting in his own body the consequences of our crimes and our sins, like a lamb going meekly to the slaughter."

This is the message which I hammered away at day after day in my meetings with Ferrandi. And so that it wouldn't sound too abstract, I remember that I said to him, "The Church is a reality which becomes flesh in the lives of Christians. Christ founded his Church so that it could become a sacrament of salvation in the world and a light for those who have lost their way, for sinners, for people whose lives have lost their meaning."

This battle of words and ideas continued for months, he with his revolutionary terrorism, and me with the Cross, where an apparent failure hangs, bound hand and foot, who does not seek to defend himself. I realized that my words often irritated him. He accused me of being too priestly.

Then one day I took my courage in both hands and

brought him a Bible, drawing to his particular attention certain passages of the Prophet Isaiah and of the 21st Psalm, the Psalm of the Crucifixion:

> He was afflicted, he submitted to be struck down,
> and did not open his mouth.
> He was led like a sheep to the slaughter,
> Like a ewe that is dumb before the shearers.
>
> Isaiah 53:7
>
> But I am a worm, not a man,
> Abused by all men, scorned by the people.
>
> Psalm 22 (21),7

"I'll leave you with these passages," I said to him, "read them when you're alone in your cell."

After several months, he asked me to hear his confession.

Here is what he wrote about our meeting, much later: "I didn't have any cigarettes, that was my main worry. Several days went by. I got to know some Colombians who were inside for coke dealing, they gave me a tin of condensed milk. I hid the lid, it had a very sharp edge, I thought about killing myself. I was already stroking my wrists. But then an officer called me, I had a visitor. It was Carmelo the chaplain. Carmelo didn't preach, he didn't ask me if I believed in God or why I was inside. He was young, small and scruffy. Well, to cut a long story short I didn't kill myself, I made my confession and I found the will to live."

I continued to visit Ferrandi in other prisons where he was sent, including Alessandria and Piacenza. And there I met other convicts. During my visits I usually celebrated Mass and afterwards I heard the confessions of anyone who asked me.

I carried on seeing them when they were under house arrest too. Many of them asked me to bless their marriages and baptize their children. And out of all this an intense correspondence developed.

I also got to know many of their relatives and the relatives of their victims.

* * *

In the letters collected together in this book, selected from the many I received, there are words of thanks to me.

But in truth it is I who should thank these young people for what they have given me, for the new perspective I have on the world, with the help of God, through their eyes.

Before I was ordained priest I was convinced that justice could only be won with violence. I thought that people who shot other people were right. I thought it was the only way to change the injustice there was in the world.

I remember once in Paris I frightened to death a Polish priest by calmly expounding my convictions to him.

This is the reason, I believe, why I was sent to London soon after my ordination. I had become a priest, but on my own terms. My gospel was Mao's Little Red Book. I was continually searching for novelty, for new experiences – like the innovative Dutch Church, for example.

I went to Holland to study it from close up. I went to Taizé, the religious community near Cluny. I spent several summers in France with Abbé Pierre, the founder of the Emmaus movement, otherwise known as the "chiffoniers", or rag-and-bone men. I spent some time at Isolotto, near Florence, where an innovative liturgy was preached. In Rome, I visited the Community of Dom Franzoni, the Abbot at the Basilica of St Paul. I was in close contact with the shanty town dwellers in Ostia. I took part in street demonstrations and in strikes. On several occasions I went on hunger strike to support their cause. In all these experiences between 1967 and 1971, I was looking for some answer that would satisfy my intense longing for justice.

At my request to be ordained deacon, my superiors invited me to leave the religious order. I was 24 or 25. They told me that I was not fit for the religious life.

In the end, after yet another meeting with my superiors, it was decided to admit me to the priesthood, but a few months later my superior told me that he regretted having allowed me to be ordained. He was profoundly disturbed by my "revolutionary" mentality.

I was sent to Ostia, to the parish church of Regina Pacis. And here the problems continued. I signed up to do a degree in sociology at the University of Rome.

At St Peter's church in London, run by the Pallottine

Fathers, one of the priests, Father Eugenio Proietti, had fallen ill, and my superiors decided to send me there to take his place. "Go to London for a few months," they told me, "then come back".

When it became known among the parishioners of Ostia that I was leaving, there was a revolt: hundreds of letters of protest were sent to my Provincial. But he would not be swayed.

I was, in fact, a terrorist. By force of circumstance, I didn't end up with a machine-gun in my hand, otherwise I would have used it. I'm certain of that. I realize now that this transfer to London was a sign from heaven. But at that moment it was a bitter punishment.

As soon as I arrived in London, I paid a visit to the headquarters of the Italian Communist Party in Dean Street near Piccadilly Circus to meet them and hear what they had to say.

I was discouraged and depressed.

I wanted to do something but nothing worthwhile came of it. And there was the language problem to cope with above all. For several years I concentrated upon the sick and the elderly.

Then in 1973, the "Way" began.

In the summer of 1973, a friend of mine, Father Giuseppe Giuli, who had come to London to study, suggested that I call the catechists of the Neo-catechumenal Community to help me. I went back to Italy and made contact with some of them. I thought they might be able to give me a hand.

When they arrived, the parish priest here had decided he didn't want them any more. What they were saying didn't seem to him to be quite suitable. So I sent them to Bedford, where they were chased away again. The parish priest decided at this point to let them return to London and agreed to accept them back at St Peter's.

As I listened to their catechesis, everything in my past seemed to become ephemeral, false, mistaken. I couldn't cope with any more of this, so I left. I went to Russia for about ten days. I don't know why I went to Russia. It was just a way of disappearing. I really wanted to ask the catechists to go, but I didn't because I didn't want to offend them. Theirs was a slow but insistent and penetrating cathechesis, a cold shower, which went on for two months until the final stage, the two-day retreat over the weekend.

In the course of that weekend, something happened which I can't explain: I collapsed, I gave in, and I saw a window thrown wide open in front of my eyes. A future which I could never have imagined. I perceived in that moment the very thing which I had spent the whole of my life searching for: a community of brothers and sisters.

The central, overwhelming issue was the revelation of the Suffering Servant, Christ the Servant, who does not resist evil. The very opposite of my own philosophy! A Christ who turns the other cheek, who washes the feet of his disciples, who takes upon himself the sins of others, who doesn't react against offence, who shoulders every burden, "considering others superior to himself, who, being God, made himself nought and became man, taking on the condition of a servant, of the lowest of this earth, obeying unto death, the death of a criminal, the death of a sinner, death upon a cross" (Philippians 2:6-8). The Christians in this world are like this, they told me. "When we are cursed, we answer with a blessing; we suffer ourselves to be hounded; we are insulted and answer courteously. We have become as the scum of the earth, derided by all men" (1 Corinthians 4:12-13).

Another important aspect of their teaching was the new light in which sin appeared to me. For the first time I realized that it is the source of all evil. I, who had desired to destroy the structures of both political and ecclesiastical power, in order to renew them, realized how useless this was if the heart of man is not changed.

On my travels, especially in the East, in India and Thailand, I met many young Europeans who had everything they desired at home, but had left everything behind them, searching for something which would satisfy them. "But what are they looking for?" I asked myself. Many of them came from Catholic backgrounds. But they hadn't obtained any of the answers they wanted from the Christianity practised by their families and their churches. I asked myself,

"What is it that we haven't been able to give these young people, that they are abandoning us?"

What these young people were saying was a challenge to me, but I found I had no words with which to defend myself.

Then, very gradually, I began to see Christianity in a new light, and realized that it has an explosive power; that Christ can be the real, true answer to the vital needs that people have. Christ is no Martian, but the Man-God who has taken all our weakness upon himself, and continues to love us even to the point of giving up his life for us.

And through this horrible death, Christ, high up on his Cross with his arms open, shows to man, shows even to that most heinious criminal stained with the unparalleled crime of having killed the Son of God, the mercy and the forgiveness of God. But God has not condemned us for this crime. In raising Christ from the dead, God has freed mankind from the slavery of the devil, conquering both death and sin.

In this sign of the Cross and in the Resurrection of Christ, everything has a meaning. In this Christian light, everything takes on a different sense. That is why the Church can offer to everyone, even to those who have had their lives totally destroyed by destroying the lives of others, this message of forgiveness.

In the Resurrection of Christ everything takes on a different meaning. You can't justify evil, but you can understand it. Someone who has killed certainly doesn't deserve medals and high honour. But it is important that the message of forgiveness reaches him too, because it can make people change their ways.

The design of Divine Mercy goes well beyond the labels which society attaches to its criminals: it announces through testimony born of suffering the message of God's love. Each one of us might perpetrate the most horrible deeds, and it is not necessarily true that the people in the prisons are any worse than we are, that they are all execrable creatures who deserve only to be put up against a wall and shot. These are people enslaved by sin, by evil, tricked by the devil, but God offers them the chance of making them-

selves new, of changing, of emerging cleansed from this
bath of forgiveness, and beginning a new life, on this side
of the prison bars, or on the other.

———

The author

Father Carmelo Di Giovanni, priest of the Catholic Apostolic
Society of the Pallottine Fathers, was born at Sangineto in the
Province of Cosenza, Southern Italy, on 3rd May 1944. He studied
in Rome and was ordained on 20th December 1970 at Frascati,
near Rome. He came to London in 1971 after spending several
months in the parish of Regina Pacis at Ostia Lido. Since 1971 he
has carried out pastoral work at the Italian church of St Peter at
Clerkenwell in London, concerning himself particularly with
assisting Italian prisoners. During numerous trips in Europe, North
and South America, Asia and Africa, he has visited prisons in
numerous countries (besides those in the United Kingdom and
Italy, he has visited prisons in Spain, Bolivia, Thailand, Hong
Kong and Macao).

The work of helping Italian prisoners in England is part of the
work envisaged by St Vincenzo Pallotti, founder of the Pallottine
Order. A Roman priest living in the first half of the 19th Century,
St Vincenzo Pallotti dedicated his life to awakening in the lay
congregation the ecclesiastical awareness of every Christian who
through Baptism becomes an apostle and a witness of Christ.

He was especially concerned to help the most needy, the poor
and the imprisoned, whom he visited in the prisons of Rome. It
was through his will that the Italian Church in London was created
shortly before his death in 1854, with the particular task of looking
after the numerous Italians who had emigrated there.

Since that time, the church of St Peter at Clerkenwell has been
greatly active among Italians and their families and at present is
a meeting point for the numerous Italian communities in London.

In the last 15-20 years, however, as the flow of immigrants
from Italy diminished, St Peter's is experiencing a new phenomenon of immigration, that in particular of Italian students and
young people who have run away from home, often off-the-rails
and with drug problems. Many of them end up in prison and
when they come out they turn to the Church for material and
moral assistance.

Marco Barbone

First Encounter

I knew about Marco Barbone from the press and television but I'd never met him. Then one day, a few years ago, I was visiting a Milanese friend, an ex-terrorist, who told me that Marco Barbone was coming to his house that morning – they were going out for lunch together – and he invited me to stay.

I remember that as soon as Marco was actually in front of me all my prejudices about him suddenly seemed meaningless. The thing which struck me most about this very young man was the openness of his look and his unaffected manners. We started to talk; then we went out alone in the car, where we talked unrestrainedly and at great length in the friendliest spirit, and suddenly it was as if I had known him for years.

Subsequently I went to visit him in Milan on various occasions and I was one of the concelebrants at his marriage. Then, I was also able to experience his reconciliation with the Church. I saw how he had moved towards the Church and the Church had received him like the Prodigal Son who returns to his father's house and is received not with insults, prejudice, sarcasm or hatred, but with open arms. Delightful too was the sense of community which we all felt during the ceremony: as if the Church that we priests represented was the head, and its limbs were all the other people close to him, all his friends who had welcomed him into the community.

Our contact became intense. Sometimes I went to the trial: he looked like a beaten dog, standing there behind the bars, with an expression of profound humility and of genuine repentance on his face.

Unlike many who have only seen the phenomenon of repentance through the mass media, I am lucky enough to

31

have had the chance to know these people in a real and intimate way, and enter into their hearts. I know how different Marco Barbone and many others are from the way they are seen by the majority of people. I realize that it is hard to understand if you don't know the people concerned, and sometimes even our position as priests is unpopular; people tend to see us almost as their accomplices, almost as if we were playing their game.

One thing which I particularly remember about Marco Barbone and which struck me profoundly was the way he always rejected the suggestion that he should take refuge abroad. "I want to stay here where I committed my crimes," he told me, "to show that I really have changed, because only facts can prove it." This impressed me a great deal, considering the risks he was running.

Letter

Milan, 15th May 1988

My dear Carmelo,

To tell you about my life over these last years seems like a huge undertaking, almost a hopeless one: so you'll understand if I'm not too orderly about it, and I'll probably repeat myself. But it's a bit like taking a photograph of a mountain stream, right now it's like this, but in a moment it'll be completely different again.

My life has changed, but that's not just because I've given up politics and I've been released and started work.... the change is mostly to do with my view of life itself.

You see, it all really started with the belief that we could change the world, without looking first at ourselves. Revolution was my vision and personal ideal, to the extent that I lost touch with my sense of human reality, especially in the way I saw myself and my friends. We were drunk with the ideology we had surrounded ourselves with. Ideology has pushed a lot of people like me into violence. We had reduced the whole question of what we wanted from life to political, ideological theorizing.

And then we all know what happened, and if you'll forgive me, I won't talk about it here. I can't forget and I don't want to forget what happened but right now I want to talk to you about something else, about how everything in my life has been transformed.

Then there was prison too, a place of anguish but also a place where you have direct contact with yourself, with your own life, and I couldn't hide myself from the voice of my conscience any longer. To tell the truth, we all tried to put off the problem a bit longer, to camouflage it once more under a blanket of political analysis, of arguments that explained everything. We talked and we tried to explain the reasons for our failure, but we used a lot of words and got the feeling we hadn't said anything, or at least that we'd left bits out. The fact is that we were still like fish in an aquarium, believing that we had a broad view of things, when we were really prisoners behind a barrier which hid from us the truths about our own lives.

Eventually, the trial came along. It probably sounds strange saying "eventually", but it was then that I began to suspect that in a man's life, truth isn't just a topic of conversation but something more than that, something different, that pervades you, possesses you and gives you no peace. I saw my friends from the past, a desolate spectacle: disagreements, bitterness and the inability to understand each other.

The breakthrough, my real Epiphany, came about by a miracle. Yes, miracle's a big word, but I don't have a better one for describing the turmoil I felt after the meeting which changed my life. I've experienced pain and mercy, condemnation and forgiveness and all this has happened because finally my heart was opened by simplicity. Out of the blue, a priest, probably the first priest I'd ever spoken to in my life, said to me: ask forgiveness.

I did and that was the beginning of the path that leads to faith. Yes, because that was how God came into my life, that was how I finally found the strength to say to myself: you have sinned and you must ask for forgiveness.

Describing it like this makes it sound almost ordinary and perhaps it is ordinary; the moment had no particular aura, almost paradoxically, exactly at the moment when I recognized my guilt towards a man whom I had unjustly struck down, I found the strength to pray, to ask for help from a Man who has now entered, for ever, into my life.

You might ask me what difference all this makes, what do I do that's any different from anyone else? But that's not the point, I don't think I do lead any particular kind of life; yes, I work to help other people like me to overcome their difficulties but the real change is keeping one's heart open and accessible to the will of God.

I've read the Miserere over and over again: the profoundest choice of my life is right there: I recognize my guilt, my constant betrayal and constantly seek to follow the truth of my life.

Dear Carmelo, I'll close now: I had my doubts about telling you these things. Above all, I believe that respect exists for those who have suffered and are suffering. To claim you've changed always makes people sceptical, incredulous. Actually, I'm telling you these things in confidence, almost in a whisper. All the same I feel I have a debt towards society and I'll try to honour it in this way: by bearing witness to a change which, since it was possible for me, is possible for everybody.

Perhaps this is the real message of faith for the world now: the heart of a man can change at any moment, every instant has eternal value because in any moment of your life, you might find the courage to open the door to Christ.

This is what happened to me.

We think about you always and we are close to you. Think about us also in your prayers.

Until we meet again very soon,

Your

Marco

Paolo Bianchi

First Encounter

I had heard about Paolo Bianchi in the Neo-catechumenal communities in Rome, I think two years ago. I phoned him, I turned up at his house and I realized that if I had heard him talked about, he had also heard about me from the brothers in the communities.

When I arrived at his house I found an enormous dog to welcome me. I immediately regretted having gone because the dog frightened me, I am terrified of dogs. Then I saw a group of young children, his and Isabella's, and all of a sudden the dog seemed very meek, it only sniffed at me.

Paolo embraced me, he introduced me to his wife Isabella and the children and asked me to stay for dinner. After a few minutes we felt as if we'd known each other for ages; a strong sense of fellowship sprang up quite spontaneously between us, with his family and with the children too, who took to me straight away. Perhaps it was also because we all shared in the spirit of the Neo-catechumenal Way. And Paolo had the same sensation too, of having known me for a long time.

His home was chaotic, what with all the children, bird cages, and this enormous dog. However, despite the chaos, I noticed a great, internal order, a profound communion, in which I saw the presence of the Lord.

Letters

Rome, January 1988

Dear Carmelo,

I am writing to you with happiness. At home whenever we talk about you, we feel so happy, and even more so when you come to visit us like last time. We couldn't have enjoyed your visit more.

Dear Carmelo, if I hadn't met men like you, I would still be a prisoner of my past and I would never have known the love and the mercy of Christ who is the light of my life.

Now, Carmelo, I am being reconciled with the world and with myself and if the Lord helps me I will succeed in this undertaking, which for me alone is impossible.

This year I also had the grace and the joy of welcoming our Lord Jesus Christ into my home with all my brothers. We welcomed Him in New Year's Eve by celebrating Mass at home, which ended five minutes before midnight. At midnight we exchanged the sign of peace and we began to celebrate, eating, drinking and playing games with the spirit that only the Lord can give. Some of my brothers and I stayed up till half past six in the morning.

How did you spend Christmas, Carmelo? We think of you constantly. I'm sending you the tape of your interview on Channel 5 with this letter. Oh, and I almost forgot. One thing you said made a big impression on me: "People aren't stupid and they can tell if you're just a professional talker, or if your heart's really in what you're saying".

Now I'll say goodbye, with the brotherly embrace of the peace of our Lord Jesus Christ.

Paolo

Rome, 25th March 1988

Dear Carmelo,
I'm a little ashamed of my long silence. Only your forgiveness can help a brother as remiss as me.

Dearest brother, I love this time of the year because there's a wonderful air of expectation just before Easter, although it's also been a very busy time for me. I'm about to open the shop and you can't imagine all the running around and the red tape, and the "made in prison" label stuck onto me certainly doesn't help things.

Marco came, and he told us (with great excitement) that you're coming over again in May. We can't wait to welcome you back amongst us again, and we have a lot of other news to tell you, apart from the shop.

Sometimes I see my wretchedness, Carmelo, and I feel far from the Lord without realizing that He is there beside me and that He loves me for what I am.

This mystery overwhelms me, it eludes me, you can't touch it and it's against any kind of human reason. I feel Jesus Christ reconciling me with other men, it's a wonderful feeling. Do you know, Carmelo, I thought I was an idealist and instead I discover I'm selfish and very materialistic, a very small man who's just looking for an easy life.

But through Christ, I can see the infinite, the eternal, and I can see how mean my life is. I wanted a beautiful house and every possible luxury, but now I can see that these things all push God to one side, I'd made Him the last of my projects. I disgust myself. I'm even worse than I was before. But perhaps the Lord is using the shop to disenchant me with the bourgeois life too, and despite all my moments of doubt and rebellion, I feel now more than ever before that outside the Church of Jesus Christ there is only darkness and death.

I hope that this Easter I will become a new man and that our Lord Jesus Christ will come to save the world.

Now I'll let Isabella add a line. I send you all my affection and love, and may the peace of our Lord Jesus be always with you and in all your works.

Paolo

Rome, 26th May 1988

Dearest Carmelo,

The further I go on my way to conversion, the more I realize the great importance that the Church is taking in my life. Without the Church I might have become worse than I was before, aggravated by my terrible experience of prison; ten long dramatic years.

But through the Church I found the forgiveness of God which has given back a meaning to my life. Only the forgiveness of God can give a meaning, though not of course a justification, to one's actions.

37

Forgiveness completely changes your viewpoint, it helps you to see other people for what they are, without judging them. Personally, I feel as if some kind of switch inside me had been thrown, and I no longer want to judge people.

Before I felt I was wicked and I isolated myself, staying on the margins of society. In prison, I couldn't find space, couldn't classify myself, I felt wretched. Then I understood the value of God's forgiveness, which is possible even after robberies and murders. Only those who forgive a person who's really done them wrong can show what God's forgiveness is, and it's genuine forgiveness, not just a strategy for staying on good terms with someone.

It is an extraordinary example and by this example you can make other people understand what a man's life has been. It's difficult to get out of the ghetto once they've labelled you.

But man is a living creature, he changes, he evolves, he can't be simply wicked or simply good. I once kept a wolf at home, a real one, it was actually a very affectionate beast, but nobody would have guessed that, given the well-known cruelty of wolves.

When God's mercy touched my heart I realized that "before" I wasn't being true to myself at all; I had worn borrowed clothes. I had been exploited by society, by my school, and especially by a teacher from the youth club in Tivoli who first got me to enter the tunnel of the terrorist adventure. When I began to see that I had got myself into a much more ambiguous environment than I had first imagined, I tried to change my life but the teacher succeeded in preventing me. From street disturbances and para-military camps I moved on to the armed struggle and robbery.

One time, I led a commando group with such ability and decisiveness you'd have thought it was the work of professionals. Shortly afterwards I was arrested. In Regina Coeli prison I turned to political activity. In the meantime, Concutelli had come to Rome and after the murder of the magistrate Occorsio, took command of the newly-formed terrorist organization GAO, the New Order Action Group.

After my release from prison, after the maximum period of preventive detention had expired, I immediately joined the new organization, and I was on the run. I was arrested again and spent 1978 in prison. When I came out in April 1979 the political situation had changed: New Order had been dissolved, the "Armed Revolutionary Units" (Nuclei Armati Rivoluzionari, NAR) had been born. By now I had become a real bandit: I carried out one robbery after another, I wanted to get us back to the kind of organization we had had in Concutelli's time but I was met with mistrust and selfishness from various small groups. During a robbery, I was captured. In prison I went on hunger strike. I was quite prepared to put an end to everything. But it was then, sick and bidding for suicide, that I began to see things in a new light. Through my suffering I understood the suffering of the others.

The books that I'd read (Evola, Guenon, Maerink etc.) talked about oneself as being the centre of the universe. Through suffering (the suffering of my family, my own suffering, the suffering I had inflicted, the suffering which became known through the press and television) I asked myself who I was, trying to understand how to position my past violence. I saw that there was no position for it, that I didn't occupy a position. I felt more and more detached from everyone who practised violence.

After the massacre at Bologna station I decided to talk, to help the investigators, when the judge showed me a photo of a child of 12 torn apart by the explosion. Then the judge took me out of the prison, without handcuffs. He trusted me. And I couldn't disappoint him. I could have run away at any moment but I didn't. I stayed to help him.

But I didn't start out on the road to redemption in prison. That began afterwards when I went back home. In prison I had just asked myself one major question: what right does anyone have to go as far as suppressing another man's life?

In right wing circles I had met with the moralism and the respectability of the self-appointed custodians of revolution who always got off everything scot free. I was a right-wing "purist", as far as I was concerned there was no difference between all the little groups preaching political revolt. I only realised much later how they had exploited me, how they'd exploited so many kids like me.

I had started in 1970, when I was 16, with a robbery at a former military depot. It was a time when we all thought of ourselves as revolutionaries, on the left and on the right. The myth of Che Guevara had a meaning for me too, and I didn't realize then that violence doesn't cure evil but if anything aggravates it.

Out of prison I realized I had changed, and I saw reality in a normal perspective not distorted by myth. I realized I had become normal when I was accepted by the others for what I was. It was the love of others which has enabled me to start again. And from my point of view, when I saw that people didn't treat me differently or more affectionately, but normally, like anyone else, I managed to put myself in other people's shoes and started to take on other people's problems, something that had never happened to me before. According to right-wing thinking, it is important to be at the centre of the universe, a superman, but I realized with the help of God, that the most important thing is to live an everyday life, working, taking care of the children, these are the real heroes, the unsung heroes.

My "dissociation" from armed struggle and my decision to collaborate with the judge investigating the Bologna massacre allowed me to meet people who fought against the perpetrators of horrible misdeeds at grave personal risk, and not always with the support of the authorities. This all helped me to make a proper evaluation of my past and I agreed to make a full confession. But Christ still wasn't there in this confession. I found Christ very gradually when I began to attend the neo-catechumenal community where my wife was already a member, encouraged by the example of a friend who came to collect me and take me to the meetings: I was under house arrest at the time. At the time of the final retreat, a weekend, my wife telephoned me to say that there had been a check by the DIGOS, the police anti-terrorism squad. "Hurry" she told me. I rushed off, but as I was leaving one of the group said to me, "I feel that you'll come back". "He doesn't realize", I thought, "that I have to stay at home to avoid trouble." I decided to abandon the community, it was too risky to go away when the police were looking for you.

But when I got home something clicked inside, "Why," I said to myself, "why should I give up this experience which I value? After all, I want only to go and listen to people talking about love." And I went back. The Brother who had said, "I feel you'll come back" welcomed me with a smile, without a word, almost as if to say that it couldn't have been otherwise. After that time, the police didn't search for me any more. At first I thought it was a lucky co-incidence but then I realized that it had been God's plan. I also experienced God's help when I was unemployed and close to despair.

Before, I had never worried about money, I had never given things much value. On leaving prison, I found I had become a father (now I have five children). I've "grown up" and I realized that the reality was much sadder than it had appeared to me at first. It was a frightening feeling. If it hadn't been for the Church, I might have got even worse than before. But instead I've realised the worth of work, the worth of a pair of hands for earning one's daily bread.

The biggest discovery for me after my joining the Community was the figure of Christ, the Christ who died for me. My relationship with my brothers and sisters and with the world is now filtered through Christ. With Christ, I am no longer afraid, I feel calm and view my past as my way of reaching him. I believe that if I hadn't had so many misfortunes, I would never have reached him.

In prison I felt alone, I felt desperate. I fell into the deepest despair. It was only after this despair that God helped me to understand that everything in my life hasn't been in vain because when one is alright one doesn't leave room for God.

In the depths of despair, I who had always been fascinated by the myth of the hero, of the superman, saw Christ as the greatest man of all, because unlike all the other heroes, he died for his enemies. This was an irresistible message for me.

Excuse the long outburst, dearest Carmelo, but I feel that I have to tell you at least a small part of what is happening to me. Pray for me as I pray for you.

Paolo

Paolo Bianchi was born in Rome on 28th July 1954. He belonged to the fierce right-wing subversive group Ordine Nuovo (New Order). Between 1974 and 1985, while in prison, he studied medicine and reached the fifth year of the course. He was charged with re-establishing the outlawed Fascist Party, belonging to an armed gang, subversive association and being an accomplice to other crimes. He is awaiting judgement in the trial of 160 accused from Ordine Nuovo. He is married to Isabella Vetrani and they have five children.

Massimiliano Bravi

First Encounter

I met Massimiliano Bravi in a special wing for political prisoners at Rome's Rebibbia Prison where I had gone to celebrate Mass one Sunday. There, amongst a small group of prisoners of various extractions, was this very young man. I remember that he came to Mass and followed it with great interest. Afterwards we spoke at length and soon established a cordial relationship.

I was told that he had been accused of belonging to the New Red Brigades. When I first saw him it gave me quite a surprise. I couldn't believe that such a young boy could be accused of being involved with an organization of that kind. He seemed to me a very straightforward, open young man. Soon afterwards he sent me a poem, the first of those printed below.

Poems

Rebibbia Prison, Rome, November 1987

A Moment

Today too, tiny chequers of sunlight
slowly chase around my cell.
On my bed, too hard for comfort, my
thirsty eyes are glued to the ceiling
whilst the thread of time
unwinds down an endless road
and hope, with broken wings
rises up, falls down again
with a thump it breaks my heart to hear.

43

I'd like to chant a song
or perhaps a lament
which would magic me up to the sky
up where the stars yell up there
in that huge emptiness
and feel
that my life's still full
and touch a little love with my hands
and forget
and erase from my memory
these cold walls
the bars
and a bed with no more dreams.

I want to chant a song
even for a single moment
because I'm one man among many
because I've fallen down
but I still won't bow my head:
I'm on my feet again, ready to fly.

Rebibbia Prison, December 1987

If you think about it
(written in Roman dialect)

Its really true you know, this really is the pits
and i'm really in it up to ere!
i wish i could kip more than just in bits
an wake up in the clear.

I'm so pissed off inside of ere
hiding wot i write from the screws
its like i'm holding hands with fear
dealing with this its seriously bad news.

I'll never come back inside this door
these walls they make me sick
i wanna think about real life once more
make love, get back to nature quick
cos you only got one life for sure
an you cant waste it in the nick!

Rome, 6th March 1988

My dear Carmelo,

It is with no slight feeling of excitement and happiness that I write in reply to your last letters, which reached me almost simultaneously at the end of the month. (I will shortly explain the reasons for this.) But first I would like to return your warm fraternal greeting, which, I must tell you, brought much happiness and peace to my heart.

Dear Carmelo, I can finally breathe a sigh of relief. I am home! Yes, I am at home again. They have finally granted me house arrest.

That's the great news I wanted to give you. Isn't it fantastic?

Finally after much suffering, faith and hope have prevailed, exactly as you always said they would.

That's why receiving your letters had such an effect on me, and why I always feel a bit shaken up whenever I think of you and remember what you're like and the things you say...

Now I feel fine, psychologically more than anything else, because as you can imagine, my mother's first concern when I got back home was to put the 4-5 pounds that I lost in prison back on me, as quickly as possible.

But joking apart, I feel very well, relaxed, calm and above all, happy to be back with the people I love.

I'll say goodbye for now, and send you all my very best love. Hoping to see you very soon, OK? Ciao.

Massimiliano

Rome, 21st April 1988

Dearest Carmelo,

I hope you're well, even if it's pointless to ask, since you sounded in great form when we last spoke on the phone!

I've finally managed to write to you after all this time, and I am terribly ashamed of myself for keeping you waiting so long. As I mentioned to you on the telephone, the last twenty days have been a total disaster. A very young friend of mine died here in my house from an overdose of drug and because of this the police accused me and my younger brother of conspiracy to manslaughter. They took us to a room in the police station and after a terrifying interrogation (third degree, with all this outrageous physical torture, electric shocks, beatings, kicks in the face, punches, etc.) they released me and my girlfriend, but they arrested my brother and charged him with pushing drugs; an unjust, unfounded and defamatory accusation which upset some people so much that they've wrecked my car in revenge, written abuse on the walls of my house, and I'm getting constant threatening phone calls and letters etc.

Now my brother Giovanni is at Rome's Regina Coeli Prison and the judges have refused him an immediate trial (which is actually his legal right for the crime they've accused him of) even though he has no previous convictions.

So you can imagine what a state I've been in recently, and you can imagine what kind of repercussions there have been at home... and that's why I took such a long time writing to you. In any case things are better now, thanks to the comfort which the re-discovery of faith has given me and above all the hope which is always with me.

Dear Carmelo, I want you to know that even talking to you on the telephone was, as always, a joy and a moment of rare serenity. Isn't that wonderful? I really owe you a lot, above all for the sense of help being at hand which I've felt inside me ever since I met you. You've managed to motivate me totally: I admire many things about you; the fact that it's so easy to communicate with you and that you're always so ready to help, are just two of the many human qualities you possess.

What more can I say to you, Carmelo? I am very happy to have had the chance of meeting you face to face, even if our meeting did take place in such painful surroundings as prison. Please don't misinterpret my words. They are straight from the heart and aren't covering up any ulterior motives. I know that perhaps I even say certain things I shouldn't, but that's the way I am: I'm not prejudiced and I'm very straight talking, if I feel something inside, I'll come right out with it.

Now I'll say good-bye. I send you all my brotherly love. I hope I'll able to meet you again face to face: it would be a great pleasure for me. Ciao.

Massimiliano

Rome, 21st April 1988

Dear Carmelo,

I'd like to tell you something about myself and about my life, following on from our meetings in prison. I am twenty-five; I was born in Rome and still live there. I was arrested in May 1987 and I am still awaiting judgement on the charges of "participation in an armed gang, possession of weapons, receiving stolen property and aiding and abetting criminal acts", following the trial of the Union of Communist Fighters / Red Brigades.

I was born in one of the many working class neighbourhoods in that old part of Rome which, even today, still bears the marks of the old misery which the War brought along.

My childhood was spent in the midst of the toils and tribulations of a large family – there were seven of us – we were poor but respectable. Then when I was twelve, my parents decided to leave the city to look for work. I stayed in Rome, bent on continuing my studies, and determined to find a means of supporting myself.

It was 1975. I found work as a porter and that enabled me to stay at high school long enough to acquire my diploma. I became an electrical technician. I felt very proud.

During the last years of the seventies, the youth revolt was broadening into public demonstrations, general strikes and into organized terrorism. This was the period in which the Red Brigades kidnapped and then killed Aldo Moro, the president of the Christian Democrats.

During this time, I started to have my first feelings of doubt too: I looked around me, and my anger at my wasted youth ignited the spark. Going to high school during those "years of lead" (anni di piombo), as they came to be called, taking part in political assemblies and collectives, meet-

47

ings in schools, or just being closer to where things were happening, it all gave me an identity and a political awareness that carried me onwards by a natural, almost automatic process, to the point where I found myself involved in an illegal revolutionary movement. And so I began to militate on the extreme Left. That led us to the first pickets outside schools and factories, the clandestine meetings, the assemblies at university, the unauthorized marches etc. It was in this particular political period that most of the terrorist activity took place, attacks on various people, knee-capping, kidnapping, fund-raising robberies, bombings etc.

I just played walk-on parts in all this, like all the other 16-18 year olds: we picketed schools, leafleted the University, organized marches; I often helped the "grown-ups" by making Molotov cocktails or carrying bags full of fuses. I was in the rearguard during the dynamite attacks on the neo-Fascist Party branches, I was in the "disturbance cells" during our unauthorized demonstrations when we wrecked parked cars, buses and shops or threw incendiary bottles to block the traffic... and we made banners and Da-Tze-Baos; we went round the city at night writing slogans with spray cans or sticking posters on walls.

This very intense period of my life was interrupted in 1982 when I was called up for my year's military service. This experience brought with it a series of events which left an indelible mark on my personality: relationships destroyed, illness, drugs, but above all the collapse of so many ideals I had defended until then, sometimes even with my blood.

That year, my whole life was in a constant turmoil, full of contradictions which utterly confused my mind: I found myself alone once again, against the world, and needing to sort out a lot of things in my mind.

I didn't know what my own identity was any more, or my life, and even less what my "politics" were. I felt drained of ideas. I couldn't find any reasons to try to improve my situation. I didn't have the strength to fight against things, and at the same time, my heaviest drug experiences happened; hashish, LSD, heroin, which I will always keep with

48

me as fearfully indelible scars on my personality and my body.

This dark period of mental chaos, only very rarely relieved by lucid moments, culminated in a terrible crisis of depression which was scarcely improved by my returning home. 1983 was drawing to a close, and it was in that period, on my return from a long convalescent break, that a kind of change or conversion happened to me.

My past adventures and experiences had evidently created a kind of platform on which the basis of a different life, a new existence was being formed. "I've finished with politics, drugs, bad company" I told myself, and this was the new slogan which had engraved itself on my unconscious mind. And in fact from 1983 onwards, my life went through a complete change.

I'd finished my military service, my physical and mental recovery were finally complete: I managed to find another job, a really excellent job which gave me a lot of satisfaction, financially too: I was working in the tourist industry which meant I could travel a lot; something which I had missed out on and which I had always been fascinated by. It enabled me to appreciate so many things that life has to offer, things I had previously ignored or simply not known the value of because I had such different interests then.

I've always been incredibly attracted by travelling and getting to know different people and places, which is why I always jumped up to volunteer when trips in Italy or abroad came along.

But the people who eventually put me in the situation I'm in now were also aware of this fact. Because several individuals contacted me during this time, through a former "comrade in arms" who had since moved on to armed terrorism. I only discovered after my arrest that they were members of the UCC-Red Brigades.

Using the weapon of friendship, they persuaded me to sub-let a room in my flat to a young couple who were to all appearances utterly respectable. Everyone knows how friendship can open doors, because it puts people off their guard. Relying on this and on the fact that I was out of the flat for practically the whole day, and often for several days at a stretch, this unimpeachable young couple, friends of friends, were at liberty to study the flat and my habits in the closest detail, as well as all activity in the neighbourhood etc, etc, despite the shortness of the stay I had allowed them – out of a more than justified diffidence. After 15 days in my flat they left, and I heard nothing more either from them or my "friend".

My life went on in the usual way, and I had a good deal of personal and professional satisfaction during the years that followed. I travelled, travelled and travelled. My morale was sky-high, and I'd got drugs and politics and other weird ideas right out of my head. I concentrated on enjoying myself and working.

But then the same person made contact again, using the same tactic of our "old friendship": this time he obtained a slightly longer sub-let from me (20 days). Once again, it was a young couple, completely above suspicion. They told me they were university students. They were friendly, well mannered, perhaps a bit too reserved (now I know why) and always willing to help out. As usual, I was never at home, completely absorbed in my fantastic job. This fact obviously convinced my two lodgers that they'd found a perfect place they could rely on if they ever needed one.

In fact, just over a year later they latched onto me again – this was in 1987, and their final, fatal visit – the usual respectable, professional couple, and this time they managed to sub-let the room from me for over two months. And as usual the couple who took the room looked and behaved irreproachably, which only served to rid me of any possible doubts or uncertainty I had about their real identity.

It must have been obvious that I suspected nothing, and thanks to this and the psychological advantage of friendship, this last couple managed to set up an operational base in my home, complete with equipment, documents, weapons etc. Unaware of any of this, I carried on innocently with my daily life, back very late every evening, going straight to bed: in the morning I had to get up very early to go to work so we just exchanged a couple of words on rare occasions, and anyway I didn't have the time or much inclination to start having conversations with them when I'd just got up in the morning.

Well anyway, I came home one evening after yet another trip, I'd been driving for three days and I was totally shattered, I just had time to put my key in the lock when I was surrounded and jumped on by God only knows how many carabinieri all in full combat gear. It all happened in a flash – I realised that it was me they were interested in, and they had me on the floor, handcuffed and stripped, and started beating the shit out of me.

There's no point trying to describe the dismay I felt, that crazy feeling of just nothing, the fear, all those thousands of sensations which invaded my brain during those endless moments: but I know all about the rage which exploded inside me in the high security cell in the carabinieri barracks as soon as I'd got my mind round what had happened.

There have been hours and days of indescribable bitterness and depression but mainly of hate towards myself and towards my own manifest incapacity to act responsibly: I'd been unable to defend my life from outside attack and I hadn't had the wit to see that I was being conned.

What condemnation is worse than self-accusation? I went to prison with that attitude, and it took away any chance of hope; and hope for what, anyway? By then I'd realised what I'd let myself in for. After five or six months of hard imprisonment and violent self-criticism, as well as a lot of self-inflicted psychological punishment, I saw a door open, and began to be aware of a weak light inside me, a way out, a new path to follow, the one that I now know for certain is a certainty: there's always hope in life. And my life has been changed ever since I took all of this on board.

My relationship with myself and with everyone else has changed, my contact with reality is different, my reactions to my surroundings have altered. Now I'm full of clarity and everything seems to operate on a more real, more human scale. There's a new man inside me, longing to make a new start, to take on the whole world, made strong by a consciousness that's enlightened, limpid, as hot as the blood flowing through our veins; and I know I've been born again, that I'm living in this world, and it's brand new to me: I know where to look, I recognise the Voice and I feel it close to me always.

It is this certainty, an inexhaustible font of security and strength, which makes me look forward with optimism, which chases away the dark clouds when they come by, and it encourages me to keep going along the right road; and it's why my imprisonment is less awful, easier to bear, and perhaps even constructive.

It has to be said that I owe all this to the moral and spiritual assistance which has been offered to me by men full of humble charity whom I met in a particularly difficult moment. I had never experienced such a feeling of profound, internal excitement simply listening to the words of another man. And yet the very message which you made me absorb as if it were an actual tangible fluid, was the spring which opened the door onto a new road for me to follow.

There's no doubt that all this gave me much cause for thought at the start, especially about its significance in modern life, in this society, where everything is based on rapid change and on the overturning of values as quickly as possible; in fact I didn't think there would be room at all for a way of life that was so different from the basic norm: a contemplative way of living, deliberately tolerant towards others. But gradually, as time passes, I become increasingly aware that only a spirit of vigilant self-criticism can give, by virtue of its placid stillness, that internal equilibrium which of all the parts of our personality able to help us through our hectic existence, is surely the most valuable.

Now as never before, I believe that the only means of salvation we have is Faith and Hope, which makes the Light shine on us, showing us a better path than the one we've followed up until now, which was the wrong one and it led us into error – look where it got me. It gives us faith in ourselves and in our capacity to become better people, and faith that we can reach this goal, and the commitment to follow it to the end, and the conviction of our own strength.

I've made a lot of mistakes in my life, and I treasure them as part of my stock of experience. But this particular experience has undoubtedly changed me in the most profound sense, as it has shown me and continues to teach me how to live each day, following the light which illuminates the path of righteousness. Yet I know that it is often very easy to make mistakes, and if we were to rely entirely on our own strength I am sure it would be practically impossible for us not to fall into temptation.

So I can only give thanks to "Him up above" for having given me the chance to see, and the opportunity of thanking him.

And to you again, my heartfelt thanks.

Massimiliano

Rome, 25th July 1988

My dear Carmelo,

I am writing to you on a relentlessly torrid day at the end of July, 39 degrees of heat crushing everything in a concrete embrace, pitilessly forcing my thoughts to return to a reality which is becoming every day more and more oppressive. I am still under house arrest, thank heavens, with the terrifying prospect hanging over me of at least twelve months' further delay. In fact I found out from my lawyer that a committal for trial has been sought on my account, on the charge of participation in an armed gang. So I can wave goodbye to my hopes that they might be looking into possible acquittal: the judge didn't even consider it for a second.

I really didn't need this! It has totally stunned me, mainly because I had hoped that fourteen months of preliminary investigations would have been sufficient for "justice" to establish the responsibility and the status of the various defendants. But it seems that this is not so!

So what is this farce? Here I am, deprived of all my rights and especially of my physical freedom, just because of the chronic maladministration of the Italian legal system. Now I fully sympathise with those people who tried to denounce the legal apparatus, ages ago. It's all got snowed

under by God knows what funny business... You know,
Carmelo, I sometimes think that life, that little I know of it,
is a play with actors, roles, plots etc, and the whole thing
is controlled by the people who are good at acting.

And I don't like it one bit! It's not real. It doesn't respect
the values that we have inside, the values which make us
human beings and not robots; straightforwardness, respect
for others and for ourselves, love etc.

Yecch! It makes me want to throw up!

OK, let's leave it at that, I'm a bit (!) depressed today.
But what about you? How are things going? I expected to
see you in June: you promised on the phone that you
would come and visit me in my humble home. Did you
forget?

I'm only joking. I know that you are very busy in your
work. How is it going, actually? Is it all proceeding in the
right direction? As I promised you (always hoping to do
something you'd appreciate) I thought I'd send you some
bits and pieces I've been writing in the last few days.

Still, I keep looking forward to seeing you and when
you do come it'll make me very happy.

Will you bring me some photos of all of those trips
you've made? Give my regards to the boys in the observa-
tion wing at Rebibbia if you should ever see them.

All my love,

Massimiliano

Poems
Two wings to fly with

I swim in the silence of this tired house
and drag myself onwards with moderation
in the torrid ritual of the succession of days.
I'm still waiting for you freedom
you'll come back to me I know –
but just now everyone has gone away:
my friends my friendships
and all those things which make this life more beautiful.
They've all gone,

the colours of the sky, of the sun and of the people;
the scent of the air and the noises of life the other life –
which pulsates and still flows despite everything –
and cynically ignores my anxiety.
I'm waiting for you freedom.
You've taken a corner of my life.
Oh what a price to pay! –
But now I know how precious you are
and when you come back
I'll have my wings again to fly with
and they'll be mine alone –
and I'll believe again and I'll fight again.
Come liberty!
Now I am paying but you will be mine again.

From house arrest, Rome, July 1988

Mirage

... July night, you set me dreaming!
But maybe
it's only the leaden sultriness
that reminds me of the sea;
and I search for you:
sea where are you?
The salt in my hair
skin hot under the sun
sand between my fingers
and your scent oh! yes your taste...
and the sound of the undertow
which sounds like songs to the sky...
and the midnight swims...
and the wild women naked, they drive you crazy...
Sea! And where is the music which inspires my thoughts...
Sea where are you?

... Absently I open my eyes
at the ring of the doorbell

and I drown my awakening
in the black ink of my biro
which already stains
the register of the two policemen.
It's time for their check:
I prisoner sign the receipt of my prison!

July night, you're driving me wild!
But maybe it's only my imprisonment
which makes me dream of the sea;
and I search for you;
where are you sea?
Closed up in the casket of my dreams you rest
and by a mirage
you assuage my rage
which is slowly consuming me
taking me by the hand
to the day of the trial.

Railway track

...And then, the country comes
flat
spread out
red hot
under the sun it lies
with no peace
ploughed into squares
by microscopic dry furrows
a memory of watered fields.
And the eucalyptus trees
all around
spread out in the unreal air
to capture atoms of life
and the vagabond eyes fixed
at the window of this train
which doesn't stop anywhere
and it's taking me
straight to where the sun dies:

in a house-jail
prison without bars
without any more words
where there is never any space
where there is no more honour.
Where there is no life.

Massimiliano Bravi was arrested in May 1987 in Rome, during an anti-terrorism operation following the killing of Air Force General Licio Giorgieri on 20th March 1987.

Viero Di Matteo

First Encounter

I met Viero Di Matteo several years ago, in Rome's Rebibbia prison. I think he was one of the first prisoners I visited there. I celebrated Mass that Sunday and he did the readings, and we talked together for the whole afternoon. I'd never seen him before but I was struck by the attentive way he'd followed the celebration, particularly when I had asked everyone present to express a thought. And I remember that he spoke. He had a solemn, almost priestly bearing, perhaps because of the profundity of his thoughts, and very expressive eyes. He seemed to speak with his eyes. He was one of the first terrorists I met with a clear consciousness of the wrong he had done, asking for no allowances to be made. Talking to him was crystal-clear, like reading an open book. Because of his severity with himself and his refusal to admit extenuating circumstances, he easily got depressed, and I had to bolster his courage; but I sensed some reticence in him, almost as if he felt himself unworthy to receive this message of forgiveness either from God or man. He felt this very deeply. He thought he was never going to be released and I gave him courage. When he got out of prison he sent me a telegram.

We've kept up a very pleasant relationship. I remember how strongly his family feeling came out in our first meeting, his love for his wife Anna and his child Daniele. He showed me their photographs. He was proud of his son and at the same time felt ashamed before him, two sentiments he feels with a strength that has always struck me.

He is a lovely soul, this boy. He has been through a very painful process and has been lucky enough to meet people on the way who have helped him to turn back to the Church as to a mother: a mother that has revived him, like a second birth. And this is a feeling which comes out very strongly in his letters.

Rome, 4th September 1985

My dearest Carmelo, my dear friend,

Thank you so much for sending me the information I asked you for about the Neo-catechumenal communities: it's an extremely interesting idea which I'd like to have a serious look at. Unfortunately the situation I'm in at the moment prevents me from any direct contact with a community and starting to follow that Way.

And I think I really need it. Like so many other people, I was baptised a few days after I was born, and received a formal, "Christian" upbringing. Until I was 11, I went to the convent school, to Mass every Sunday, I was catechized, had my first communion, confirmation... as I say, a formal, "Christian" upbringing: and that's not a judgement, believe me, I really have no desire to criticise anyone now, it's just a statement of fact. In fact the real values which I became acquainted with, my real upbringing, were exactly the same as my parents had received, and came from their own experience of their own lives: an upbringing founded on the successful affirmation of the self – egoism, really – on the enormous importance of money, on social careerism, on the pre-eminence in one's life of a job which produces material wealth and personal "freedom", on the practising of an absolutely individualistic and basically formalistic/ritualistic religion, etc. etc.

Their all-embracing "ideal" was to be "respectable", in other words to be "polite to others" (basically, not give a damn about anyone), to "aspire" to a good social position, and, in order to achieve this, to fulfil all one's socio-civic-religious "duties". When I was about 13, I realised that actually it wasn't totally essential to go to church in order to be a good citizen. So I stopped going, and I concentrated on my studies and gained, to my parents' great satisfaction, reasonably good grades.

1968 came along; I was 16, really only just out of the nursery. I remember how keenly I listened to history and philosophy lessons, my father talked a lot about politics, and these two facts, combined I expect with something in my character, made me very attentive to what was going on in the world at that time.

For instance, the Vietnam war and the mass youth protests against "authoritarianism", for greater civil liberty, etc. For some years I had been reading the political columns every day – mainly the foreign items – in the daily paper my father bought. So, during the first weeks of the '68-'69 academic year, my "conversion" to Marxism happened. Then a rapid succession of massed student demonstrations, then assemblies, then meetings, and then demonstrations again... all without a moment's respite. In two or three years I ran away from home 7-8 times. We scrutinized all the "injustices" – the ones we experienced in our own lives and those on the other side of the world – we weighed them up one by one, inveighed against them in every possible way and with all the ardour of our excitable youthful imaginations. The thing that amazed us wasn't just having discovered what and where the "rot" was, but "knowing" how to resolve all the ills of this world. You must remember the atmosphere of those years too, Carmelo. The struggle for liberation in the Third World, the trade union protests in the Autumn of 1969, the massacre at Piazza Fontana etc. etc. And the slogans: "Workers and students together in the struggle", "Imperialists out of Vietnam", etc. etc. I switched between several different organizations of the extraparliamentary left during those years: in any case their "vision of the world" was the same: they all had the same ideology and the same proposals for the liberation of mankind: the Marxist-Leninist (with reformist-gradualist elements incorporated in varying degrees, or conversely, "revolutionary" elements, advocating the violent seizure of political power).

After two years of living together Annamaria and I got married in 1976, and the following year we had a son, Daniele. I saw him being born, you know. Usually (often? – it should be) the birth of a life (especially a human life) should constitute a moment of profound reflection and a consequent conversion to "life", to love, to co-operation. When a child is born, a man "stops" for a (long) moment and reflects on his own past and his future. Perhaps because he feels that there isn't just him to think about now, but this new life too, and he is obliged (and it really is an obligation) to be responsible for it. A son is born and you basically draw up an existential balance-sheet between your "having been-ness" and your present "have to be for him-ness". I'm sorry, I can't explain it better than that. Now I see the birth of Daniele as a tremendously wasted existential opportunity.

At least for his sake, I should have re-examined my whole past life point by point (and ruthlessly too, with respect to my personal needs for "coherence" and self-satisfaction, of role and identity). And I didn't. I went charging on, true to my identity/self-image as if driven by absolute necessity (and in the end, involving even him in all the suffering that was to come).

All those illusions, that will for power, the huge arrogance of thinking I understood the truth about the world, led me in 1978 (10 years after the start of it all) to enter the ranks of the armed struggle, i.e. of terrorism. The ideals of justice turned into murderous violence directed against the men who represented the State (the human being totally crushed in his social role) and in our eyes they were the guardians and perpetrators of every possible injustice and social suffering. They were "the unjust", we were the "avengers". A handful of terrible years, and there are plenty of victims and ruined lives to prove it. My interior life was practically annihilated by it all: communication with Anna and my friends was reduced to nothing. Each day I said goodbye to my son without knowing if I would ever see him again, my daily routine was just a devastating, breathless race... and then a feeling of loneliness which increased as, gradually, failure dawned on us. A feeling of wasted lives...

At the beginning of 1981, I left the organization (the Red Brigades) but most of the worst had already happened, to me and to many others. I spent a year organizing union activity in my workplace (I was a nurse in a hospital) but inside I knew I had no prospects any more, or any real meaning. It was an attitude left over from the past that didn't realize it was dead. With Anna discord had reached a peak and through my fault she suffered greatly. At times, often, I was like an animal.

All this was interrupted by the arrest of Anna on 1st March 1982 and me going into prison on the 5th.

And finally, these years in prison. What can I tell you about them? About the desperation, nostalgia, regret, anger, hope, the curse I have suffered between these walls? It's a world that you know well. I don't think there's any point in me dwelling on it.

The only important and decisive thing, I think (and hope) is the discovery of the word of Christ. In the end, over and above the necessity of satisfying human justice, this will be the only true significance of the years that I've spent and still have to spend in here. But it really will be like that, and one day I will be able to say, realistically, without any exaggeration, "Blessed are those chains"!

But that's exactly where a preliminary basic question arises inside me: Is that tiny faith that I'm already talking about really authentic? Is it really a little echo, inside me, of his voice or is it just a clever manifestation of my damaged ego, trying to get itself reinstated and legitimised once again? Or is it more down to earth, a need for consolation?

Try to understand me, dear Carmelo, after what's happened to me in the past, how can I trust myself? Yes, now I feel love towards the person of Jesus Christ, I believe that through him there is salvation for all men and so I would like to actually live his word each day, but at the same time, I ask my innermost self if this love, this faith and this will are really genuine and not just an elaborate projection of my own ego. The thought that this may be true makes me suffer a good deal. If it were, I would be deceiving not just myself but other people whom I respect and love, you among them. So keep this in mind. I don't know, but I think it will be difficult to overcome this doubt as long as I am still inside here. Do you think this need for being certain of the authenticity of one's faith is, so to speak, legitimate?

On the other hand, in that book by Zevini that you sent me, I read this: "... Convinced that faith is not something that we can give ourselves unaided, it is not moralism nor the fruit of our efforts; it is a gift that God gives us through Baptism." If this is true, then I haven't "discovered" anything at all, since the word of Christ would have always been in me, ever since that far off day 33 years ago when I was baptized in the font of the Basilica of St Paul outside the Walls. And the seed of Christ would have been present within me all along, even if it had lain hidden all these years, and only now it begins to germinate, now that the blind arrogant ego which smothered it has been crushed by that enormous existential failure which I have tried, briefly, to describe to you.

That must be it, mustn't it, Carmelo? I really hope so. But I still have a major difficulty, if it is true that what Zevini says is true – "Faith cannot be experienced individualistically. It develops and matures within the Christian community. It is within the communal experience that the vocation of the individual comes to light, and there too that the preconditions for fully discovering oneself and one's personal aims in life are satisfied; and thus each person also becomes a message of salvation for others". What should I do? I don't know, I think the only answer is to wait, as trustingly and serenely as possible (but in practice this is very difficult) until I am out of this wilderness, and to continue to listen to the Word, hoping and praying that it will continue to grow.

In any case, I am not really alone, if I can count on your friendship and on that of the other priests who in these last two years have visited us weekly, to celebrate the eucharist and the word. I have seen the Lord profoundly present in them. So I can't complain I'm being abandoned. On the contrary! I must pray sincerely, "He has stooped down to me, He has heard my cry for help. He has pulled me from the pit of death. He has put a new song in my mouth, praise be to God!"

I was telling you before about my "damaged ego" but believe me, "damaged" doesn't begin to convey the idea. In fact, my ego has experienced something very like death, the removal of every horizon, of every hope, of absolute cynicism, of despair. And isn't that being dead, even if you are still biologically alive? Basically, the biological being looks after itself and ends itself too. And this was exactly when He burst in... a large part of me feels that this is reality. But it's still an internal reality, with all its contradictions, its conflicts, torn between the old, the new and... nothing. Perhaps there's a relationship with the unresolved past, and a very unclear future (despite this faith that I feel), both fused together in this present which I can only just cope with and barely live in at all.

I'll give you an example of my relationship with my past: inside me, I remain keenly attentive to the problem of social justice. Or rather than attentive, I am really and truly anguished by the immense moral and material suffering of millions of our brothers (near and far) in the world. And again I ask myself, why? Can absolutely nothing be done? What effect does the word of Christ have on the alienated lives, the very real cross that these millions and millions of poor people have to bear? In what sense does it set them free?

I too believe that loving one's "enemies" is the most remarkable fact of Christ's gospel. This fact frees man from hate and gives him new life, but what does it mean in practice? I mean, for example, in the lives of men whose most sacred and fundamental human rights are not even recognized by other men? I think of the masses in Africa, in the favelas of South America, of the millions of social outcasts in the West. Aren't they more than anyone else the crucified Christ of our time? In the Acts of the Apostles, it is written, "The multitude of believers was united, heart and soul; no one claimed for his own use anything that he had, as everything they owned was held in common".

If all Christians lived like that we would truly be at the threshold of a new era. Don't you think?

But it is also true that to live like he lived, you need to be able to reject the thousands of idols of this world (to be disobedient towards the world?), you basically need to be willing to love as he loved. Right to the bitter end. You have to really die and be born again, because little adjustments, or even big ones, are certainly not enough.

I hope that it will be like this for me too.

Now I'll say goodbye, dear Carmelo. I already feel you are a very dear friend. I look forward to your reply (take your time, I have plenty of it...)

What did you mean when you said that you were reconciled with an aspect of your history by going to New York? The photos were marvellous – thanks.

All my best wishes to you,

Viero

Rome, 7th December 1985

Carmelo, my friend,

I hope you're having a peaceful and happy time this Christmas, and I send you my very warmest wishes.

Here the atmosphere is peaceful and especially serene, thanks to the Christmas spirit and also because our group is getting smaller: in fact three of us have been released (another three) because the time limit for their (precautionary) custody pending trial has expired.

From what I hear, I should be released too (for the same reason) in mid-February. I think that I might make myself useful with the little nursing skill that I have. On the other hand, the best possible thing for me would be if I could live in a community where everything is shared out with outcasts (because sharing balances out the evil of their rejection by society), and trying to follow the way that Jesus has shown, with every ounce of my strength – which is far too little on its own.

If I trust in the Lord's help it will be a beautiful period of my life, full of valuable lessons. Then I'll have to go back to prison to complete my sentence... It is my cross, dear friend, with the only (certainly not insignificant) difference that I have done everything possible to deserve it... And I even complain about the evil consequences that I myself caused: if I had known then what I know now, then it really would have been madness, but I didn't. I mistook evil for good, the spirit of this world for a spirit of love and true brotherhood and it's still hard for me to try and understand how it could all have happened.

Recently, I've been asking myself this: if a man's old self dies during Baptism and he is born again as a true disciple of Christ, "by water and by spirit", then how is it possible that I was baptized, and yet could stray so far and get so completely lost, and for so long? This contradiction (between

65

being baptized and losing one's way) has led me to conjecture that baptism cannot "work" (as a sacrament of salvation) unless it is the free choice of a man who accepts with love the living grace which God grants "from above, unto the men that He loves". But how can this be possible if the man is a newborn baby, just a few days old? ...I think it becomes a bit of a formality in these circumstances...

You know I had hoped that you would come and visit us but I wasn't surprised when you didn't come.

I pass the time reading and studying a little. I've ordered a volume of commentary on the Gospel. I hope it helps me to understand (given also the relative isolation in which I find myself) the word of the Lord better, a word which in my stupidity and smallness I regarded for years as childish, simplistic and "not enough".

My son is well. Anna my wife is fairly okay. So I'm reasonably happy. Thank you for the beautiful photographs. They are really wonderful. When you have time, call or write, OK? Let's hope that 1986 will bring more peace in the world – let's pray for this.

Yours, Viero.

P.S. By the way, isn't there a magazine or periodical about the Neo-catechumenal communities? If so, I'd like to read it. Everyone sends their love.

Rome, 28th February 1986

Dear Carmelo, dear friend,

I received your "gift-pack" with great pleasure and I'm really glad that you are well and in fine form. Believe me, your words and the reading material which you sent me are like a blast of oxygen for me, like a good medicine, like those gentle words which our mothers said to us as children when we suffered one of those (little) upsets which already happened in our lives. Today the upsets are far more serious, the trials we endure much harsher... so that an earthly mother is no longer enough to help us overcome it all. In fact mothers, as well as fathers and children, badly need help from above to escape from evil, not to be conquered by it.

By an evil which I have discovered within myself, predominant and powerful... I thought I could fight against injustice, but now I discover that I'm terribly unjust, and that makes accepting myself very difficult, even more difficult than loving others.

One thing's certain, I'm tied up with other people in one single tangled knot...

Sometimes I am strongly tempted to stop analysing myself, stop being so negative, but I believe that I would fall into the much greater sin of superficiality. And God knows how superficial I've been. It is written, "Blessed are the pure in heart" and I wonder if I will ever be blessed... The Gospel is like a mirror and it sometimes makes me feel very low looking at myself in it. But it's also true that Christ seeks out and turns towards people like me and so I try, although it's an effort, to trust in his love. I say it's an effort, and I know how absurd that is because there should be no "effort" in trusting in a God who loves you unconditionally, for free.

It must be a question of faith, I think, since mine is so frail. Even so, he must truly love me if he lets someone like me know him, or for example if he lets me enjoy your friendship which is also offered for free and not easily "justifiable".

In a few days I should be out of here (but not for good, of course... then I'll have to come back in again). I'm not absolutely certain about all this (how could I be?) but it should work out that way. I'll go where I told you I would.

Otherwise, everything's the same as usual here; exercise, reading, television, work, prison visits. On Sunday there's Holy Mass. Perhaps in a few years I'll be able to come to London but it's out of the question in the near future. Pity! But basically being in prison isn't my worst problem. I mean, sooner or later it'll be over and considering that I'm quite young anyway, it won't take too much time.

For the time being, I hope that you will come and see me when you happen to be in Rome. But I do realise that your activities over there take up a lot of time and effort and have to take priority over holidays and whatever other personal trips you might want to make.

You know that the book "Love, death, resurrection" had a deep effect on me: I see that it's part of a book published by "L'Amore Misericordioso" which I've never heard of before. Could you send me a copy? Or do you think I can find it in an ordinary bookshop? Goodbye for now, my dear friend. May the Lord Jesus keep you. I'll be thinking of you.

Viero

Rome, 7th May 1986

My dear friend Carmelo,

I really am still here. I am still stuck like a fly on flypaper with all the bureaucratic red tape (the fiscal checks). I've been waiting for the Court ruling for about three months, so I suppose it's reasonable to hope that my release is imminent.

So long as they don't find out I've inherited about 30 oil wells in Texas!

How am I? Not bad. You know, I think the main risk in these situations is visiting my own ill-humour and irritability on the people around me, and the anguish which sometimes grips me. You could easily become a burden on the people who have to live with you, communicating only your bitterness and weariness.

I don't say that I'm completely immune from these outbursts, but with the precious help of our Lord I have so far managed to retain a certain serenity and openness.

"He" is not an abstract and distant ideal; he is a "person" near to me, my own (and everyone else's who knows and loves him) matchless, utterly faithful, good friend. Sometimes I can understand and tell myself, "Whatever happens, God is my friend. He will never let me down; and so everything will be all right in the end, somehow or other."

Oh Lord, above all else, give me greater faith!

Goodbye, dear Carmelo, with all my love.

Viero

As ever, if you come across any material about the Neo-catechumenal communities, send me a copy. Okay? If I do get out before June, I'll let you know straight away.

Rome, 26th May 1986

[Telegram sent on the day of his release]

I am out. All my love.
Viero

3rd March 1987

Dear Carmelo,

Apart from a touch of flu all three of us are... flat out on the bed!

No, I'm joking! We're actually okay.

In July/August the three of us should be going back to live near Rome, so I think it'll be much easier for you and me to keep in touch.

So my "monastic life" will carry on until next summer.... I do very little work (almost none), a lot of reading, and I spend most of my time with my wife and my son. But then, we haven't been together like this for years.

In a few days time I'll be in Rome for the trial: I will be questioned by the magistrates.

I am relatively calm.

Dear Carmelo, thank you for the photos. I hope to see you soon somehow. Goodbye, my dear friend, and all my love.

Viero

14th July 1987

Dear Carmelo,

I hope that you are well, dear friend, and still the same happy and optimistic person I often recall. How can I sum up these last seven months? I've simply existed.

But is life really that simple? With all your experience,

you know it isn't. There's no joy or serenity so free and pure that it's not immediately tempered (I don't say obscured)... by anxiety, worry, egotism, pain.

No one is righteous before Him!

And this broad background of discontent is made up of thousands of tiny, only just discernible "lapses in quality", and a certain sense of dissatisfaction and sadness is simply the clearest symptom of them. And of course these "lapses" are sometimes not that small at all... as you very well know.

But I really don't want that to make my life sound dismal and joyless. On the contrary: Anna, Daniele and I are discovering daily the joy of experiencing together all the things that each day brings.

Trying to share everything, even thoughts and hopes, is the most important thing of all.

I don't have a stable job yet, and I'm getting by as a private domestic nurse (pompous name): little jobs here and there, in other words. For the moment, we've got enough money. Anna is also doing odd typing jobs.

I go to prayers with the nuns once a week and try to read and meditate on a passage from the Scriptures every day. I was interrogated in March, Anna in April. Excuse the enormous delay. And write!

All our love,
Viero and Anna

P.S. If you come here before August, we'll be delighted to put you up! After that we're moving, I don't know where just yet.

5th September 1987

Dear Carmelo,

I got the letter you wrote to me after your trip to the Far East. I am glad that you're well and keeping so busy. I haven't had much to do recently, in fact I didn't have before either. The plain fact is that I can't find a job. Our friend is very busy on my behalf, bearing in mind that with my past I can't get work through the normal channels, but the results of his efforts are still very uncertain (in a week or so I should get an answer).

And time is running out... because there are certain practical issues to do with work (like a house, since I have to leave this one) and enrolling my son Daniele at school (Form 5, he is 10 years old).

The book sounds like a good idea to me; it could be useful for people who work every day with outcasts, and even more so for raising awareness amongst those who want it in the government departments which carry the burden of making practical decisions about certain very serious problems, prison, drugs, terrorism, work, unemployment.

How often have judges judged without "knowing" either the people they were judging or the sentence to which they were condemning them? Can justice exist when we have no knowledge of our fellow men or of reality? I have been a judge too. But here we should be talking in far broader terms and perhaps reflect on the impossibility of true justice in a world where love itself, that true love founded on self-sacrifice and not on mutual pleasure, is infinitely rarer than the frequent use of the word (by everyone, including myself) might suggest.

Why should the rich and powerful give what they have to the weak and the poor? Why should they do something so unpleasant to themselves if not (sacrificing themselves) for love? How long, O Lord?

We send you all our love,
Viero, Anna and Daniele

5th May 1988

Dear Carmelo,

My warmest wishes to you. I hope that you are really well. Thinking over what I have written to you between September 1985 and September 1987 I realise that it is evidence of a shift from a life in which I didn't hear the word of God to another whose significance is completely hidden and at the same time to be sought in God, by listening to his word and putting it into practice.

These verbs, looking, listening, practising and praying define the present direction of travel in my life, of the days which I pass with my companion and my son. Otherwise, we live with the same problems and joys as many other families; Annamaria's job (the one she doesn't have!), Daniele growing up much too fast, the practical everyday things, our free time together, etc. etc. Annamaria, although she's not a believer, is very close to me in this journey of faith I'm making...

Certainly, if I look back I feel like a survivor, a ship-wreck, and it really has been a terrible storm... and I've outlived myself too, or at least a large part of me which is dead. An internal part, yes, but it was no less alive and influential for that, since it made me do all that I did.

And now how can you say to a man whose brother was killed, "Forgive us, we made a mistake..." It is an incredibly difficult situation... And yet we did make a mistake, when mistakes just shouldn't have been made about something like that...

Picture a Nazi working in the concentration camps. A fascist soldier of the Republic of Salo who takes part in reprisals and round-ups against the partisans and the population... taking part in shootings etc. They kill because they have a great ideal! ... and then realise that they have made a mistake! How inadequate and insubstantial this word "mistake" is for expressing the real, the terribly real enormity of what has happened! On one side, real blood (and lots of it!) and on the other, a noun!

Like the pilot after Hiroshima saying, "I made a mistake!"

Unfortunately there are many good examples one could give. And now, a survivor of those events, an outcast from society, I suspect I have an indelible mark upon me and I wander around the streets with a hidden fear that someone might notice it... But I hope and will endeavour to make sure that the memory doesn't become a malignant sickness... because it is good to remember: it is vitally important to remember!

I'm sending you, dear Carmelo, a declaration of dissociation from the armed struggle which I wrote in December 1983. I had just been transferred to Rome from Bad' e Carros prison in Sardinia (a year and a half there). You're welcome to read it. Even if some of its contents are dated and others (my whole experience of faith) not yet present, I think that you might find it interesting, and it may help you to a better understanding of what I have been through.

In love and friendship, all my best wishes. Hoping to see you again soon.

Your friend

Viero

Piero Falivene

Piero Falivene was introduced to me by some of his ex-terrorist friends in Rome at the Opera don Calabria shortly after he came out of prison. His friends had told him about me and our meeting was simple and friendly right from the start, with no impediments. I immediately saw him as a deeply religious person. I was struck by his serenity, and by how well he had managed to re-integrate himself in the world of work. I also saw in him, as I have in many of these boys, the great difficulty he suffered from: enormous suffering caused by talking about the past, like a wound being opened again. He was aware of the evil he had done, of having been the cause of suffering, not out of a cowardly desire to forget, but with a gaining internal awareness, the same sentiment expressed by David when he exclaimed, "My sin is always before me." And a profound desire for the Lord's mercy, to be renewed by him. In him more than anyone, I saw the clear awareness of evil and the desire to change.

Letters

Rome, 2nd February 1988

My dear Carmelo,

How difficult it is talking about the past, I won't deny that I've tried to get rid of it fast, but it's not always that easy. Those years. A collective dream, a blast of rejuvenating wind in the face of society. Just think about it, thousands of kids going out into the streets to fight for a better life, and finding there were so many of them, all with the same problems.

Almost all of us came from the outskirts of Milan, a concrete, nowhere for people to meet, or if there were any they were, just the porn cinemas. We were held down by authoritarianism of every kind, in the factory, at school, by the political parties. And then we all went crazy, our chains got broken, we poured out into the maze of the affluent society. What they said was true: the poor got poorer and the rich got richer. The deaths of our "comrades", knowing or if you like discovering that there were 6000 fatal industrial accidents a year in Italy. And other stories like that. And you were there in the middle of it all, asking yourself why and what you could do about it. The mounting anger! And in the end, the years of terrorism which were such a total disaster for so many of us. And I want you to know that terrorism didn't just destroy the families of the victims but our families too. The cry of mothers from one side mingled with that of the mothers on the other side; fathers and mothers and brothers divided by choices which we forced them to make. What a tragedy those years were. How could you want to forget it, it's just totally impossible. It's like a film they put on 365 days a year, to make you remember, so your memory can't wipe it out. You can try but it's just impossible. People say that time heals wounds but I don't believe it's true, time doesn't heal anything. What are we going to tell our children? That we killed, wounded, kidnapped people? Why? Perhaps even we don't know why, we're still hiding behind those readymade slogans we use.

I'll leave out prison. I really don't want to think about it. Just one thing. Yes, I discovered that you can't take away a man's freedom, and when I say freedom I also mean the freedom to live and not to die.

Then, when I got out, I approached religion, but it filled me with horror and I ran away again. I felt as if I was going to fall into another kind of dogmatism. And so I wandered around a bit in the maze of my memory, I tried to carry on like that. But it wasn't enough. I met a lot of priests and I noticed that none of them tried to impose their faith on me. Now it's my faith too, in a troubled kind of way; sometimes it feels like a torment and I want to run off, stop hearing people talking about God all the time. But when it gets into you it's difficult to chase it away. You know that I'm living in a religious community now.

It is a community which fills me up and gives me something new every single day. You know, I'm glad that I have changed and that I've found out that God is there beside me. I often ask myself where I would have ended up if I hadn't anchored myself in this community, or what I really mean is gone back to live in the house where I was a child.

Personally I believe that people need to understand how finding God can change you. It's so difficult, Carmelo. In the old days I would have been really outraged, I suppose the right word would be rebellious. I don't know if I have changed, I honestly couldn't tell you if I have and anyway, you know, I really can't understand why repentant terrorists (what a miserable bunch we are) always have to show our detractors that we've changed, that we really have repented. So, what else can I tell you about, Carmelo, my old pal?

Personally it's been a fantastic and amazing experience, but mainly it's been wonderful meeting the people who helped me to know the Lord. I'll pray for you, Carmelo, but you do it for me too. Let me know when you come to Rome. I embrace you in the name of our common faith.

Many and various are the things I want to tell you. For the moment I'll leave off here. So see you soon in London. May the Lord protect both of us. See you.

Piero

Piero Falivene, 25 years old, was born at Pianora (Bologna). In 1976 he moved to Milan. Arrested in 1981 in Milan for subversive association, and for having a role in organising an armed gang. Found guilty of having formed the "Antonio Lo Muscio Brigade" and "Gruppi di fuoco per il comunismo". Also found guilty of belonging to Prima Linea and to COCORI (Communist Revolutionary Committees). He repented after the assassination of the brother of Patrizio Peci, the first Red Brigade terrorist who repented and collaborated with the authorities.

Sante Fatone

First Encounter

I believe that my first encounter with Sante Fatone took place at the special security block (bunker) in Milan, near the prison where the trials were being held. I had gone there to visit Mario Marano and some others. Afterwards I visited him regularly in prison in Bergamo.

The first thing I noticed about this reserved and very timid young lad was that he never said more than he had to, it seemed as if he was frightened of speaking. I don't know whether it was out of fear of people judging him or of being misunderstood but his past was a source of great suffering for him. The thing that struck me about him was that his face was nearly always sad and his eyes expressed more than his mouth did. It almost seemed as if the events of his life (and his past) were crushing him.

At the beginning it was hard work communicating with him. Dialogue was almost non-existent, until one day something clicked inside him, and I realised that this boy had a lot to say, he had wonderful feelings, deep down he was good, with a highly remarkable inner richness. But it was hard getting into him, like breaking into an iceberg. Then very gradually he started to open up, like water streaming from a fountain.

Another characteristic of his was the great difficulty he has had in returning to society and becoming accepted by it once again.

Letters

Bergamo, 2nd August 1986

Ciao Carmelo,

I was very happy to receive your long letter. I've often tried to write to you but I never knew how to start... how

77

to finish. Well I'll try to tell you a bit about me and tell you what pops into my head every now and again.

The problem, apart from the physical one, is communicating with people and society.

Fortunately I've got a family and friends who have helped me a lot to understand the mistakes I have made and for about two years now I've managed to have a certain rapport with them which I had broken off when I was 19, around 6-7 years ago.

It's been really lovely because apart from politics and related appurtenances I've been given affection and dialogue which has helped to free me from my ideological shackles and is also helping me to cope with prison life a bit better.

The other day I was watching a rock concert on TV plus related interview with the singer, and what the bloke was saying about politics really made me listen, namely that it was time to start thinking more about people for what they are, and try and understand that we all need each other, without "big political schemes or violence". Well, I thought that was a really great thing to say, in a way I've associated it with your long letter; it would be great if we all understood each other a little better, perhaps the world wouldn't be so screwed up.

Thanks a whole load for saying you hope I'll find a job and fit back in the world outside, I would be really happy if something like that could happen; what can I say, let's hope it does.

I do understand the wrong I've done and lots of others do too, that's why I hope people will feel some pity for us. But right now prison, apart from the best will in the world, is not the ideal place for re-educating and re-integrating people who've made mistakes.

I'll finish these lines so as not to repeat myself and also because I don't really know what else to tell you now; I'll draw you some postcards and send them to you soon.

See you soon. Lots of love, bye.

I hope you can make some sense of this 'ere papyrus. Everyone else here in the wing says hi. Bye.

Sante

Bergamo, 18th November 1986

Hi Carmelo,

I got your letter with the newspaper cutting and I was very glad to receive it.

To tell the truth, I wanted to write to you before, but then, I couldn't think of anything to say, things have been slightly weird for me recently.

I've been tried in Rome for some fortunately not very serious things and they've refused me house arrest and everything else; still I'm fine, by which I mean that I'm seeing things for what they are, and anyway I'm conscious of what I got up to and that helps me.

Apart from everything else, it's all been pretty busy round here, things seem to be going quite well especially the new laws which if they are administrated properly could be a real turning point in the current "prison mentality", by which I mean they might finally start trying to re-educate people, instead of just punishing them and leaving it at that.

For example, they've already started building a new floor here, so as they could house people with minor sentences, and could enable them to benefit from a semi-detention scheme, this being important because many young people by spending all day in prison just end up learning new skills for their criminal "careers".

As for me, I've started finding out some information about something regarding a possible job outside, but it's going to take a bit of time; in the meantime, I'm trying to go on a course which the district authority does for dissociated ex terrorists, on the problem of aid for the elderly and handicapped persons. I say trying because it is a course just for "dissociates" and unfortunately there are still problems between, shall we call them, "categories" of ex terrorists. Well, as soon as I think of something to tell you, I'll write again. All my love. Ciao.

Sante

Bergamo, 13th December 1986

Hi Carmelo,

I wish you a peaceful and happy Christmas. I'm okay here, unfortunately it always takes a bit of getting used to, but apart from that things seem to be going okay, all things being equal, getting a job seems to be a prospect which could finally re-integrate me: one certainly needs patience and "luck".

Here we've just had Mass with some "dissociates" (Laronga and Fornoni) and I hope we can meet up again, do it at Christmas too. See you. Love.

Sante

Bergamo, 30th December 1987

Ciao, Carmelo

I think the problem of political prisoners is important but, once it has been pulled to bits by all the various ideological assumptions, it is still basically a problem to do with the community of men and whether they know how to live together or whether they don't.

I know that living with people is difficult, but sometimes I do think however it is something that's attainable by behaving better, to other people and to yourself, I think this without being ingenuous or arrogant.

Really if we were all good, or tried to be, I think things would have been better; the way things are in the world now is the result of discrepancies, sufferings, etc. accepting them as such is the only way for things to get better. Hope's what you need.

My news, briefly: I've been given home leave, no luck with the job, now I'm studying and more than anything else it helps to "cheer me up" from what it means to be in prison, even though it's nothing compared to the Asian countries you've told me about. But right now I'm fairly busy dealing with some not very pretty situations. I feel a bit, you know, not right in my head, but nothing to worry about... On the one hand I realize that I've gained a lot in the last few years, just understanding my mistakes. I'm sure they're all things that lots of young people in modern cities have "in common", with all their internal and external human contradictions.

Maybe I'm a bit "complicated" the way I express myself, sorry.

I'm always happy to hear your news, I'll write again soon. Love.

Sante

Bergamo, January 1988

Dear Carmelo,

I wish to tell you briefly about what my life's been like so you will know me better.

I was born in a council block on the outskirts of Milan. Today more than before, it's a city within a city, block after block of flats, wide avenues like motorways which are sometimes tricky for the children who have to cross them.

I lived there until I was 19, then I was on the run because I was wanted for being in an armed gang and other things, this went on for about 5 years.

All the contradictions I went through in those early years of my life still form the sum total of the good and bad experiences in my existence. In fact, first when I was on the run and then in prison I went through some fairly deep thinking, though during both these periods I felt pretty helpless too.

Districts full of immigrants, workers, kind of dormitory suburbs with no other facilities for a humane existence which are typical of cities in the north (of Italy). The only oases were the Oratories: those two churches with their little football pitches which offered a certain amount of recreational space, you could play there. When I got older I started to see with anger the squalor of those dormitory suburbs.

I went to high school and at the end of it I got my diploma, but I didn't make the best of my time then anyway. It was the time when the authorities in response to student pressure had introduced obligatory passmark for all who attended school. So that was how I passed. School wasn't too important for me then, and I was interested in other things.

I was made very angry by all the hypocrisy which I experienced too, in Milan itself, outside of my neighbourhood.

There I went around with people like myself and quite soon we were deep into politics. We were left wing, at times you might say even in a sort of folksy way. We joined other collectives, workers groups, because we felt that this was necessary for bringing about changes. We wanted to change more or less everything, even relationships between people. All wonderful thoughts, except that the air was full of smog and peculiar ideas championing the coming of the power of the proletariat...

I along with some of the others tenaciously progressed towards our ideal which it was clear that nobody really understood but it was an ideal all the same. I don't want to sound pathetic but there is such a thing as diminished responsibility, I mean sometimes it's more of an instinct that guides you rather than reason. The dream was enticing but it was arduous and looking at it today with hindsight one might say it was raving mad. I wanted to change things instead I might just have helped to make things more complicated. Our wanting to be equal was dictatorship. The fact we got on well together was just because of our collective search for affection, and it was all infected by the constant political pressure.

I've always tried to win respect for me and other people, but then our ideology helped to trample on this instinct, we used violence to build our power. We were never going to resolve any problems, we would have just built a closed society and we certainly would never have restructured production methods. Experience teaches, historical experience to be precise. I think contradictions in society have to be answered with dialogue, up to the point of exhaustion if necessary, and this is true even for the smallest little daily problems, only in this way can people grow and try to be helpful to others.

What I would like to repay to society today, for there

are atrocious events and deeds which I wouldn't know how to repair, is to be able to express and explain this transformation in myself and make it possible for me to be useful to others and myself. It's an open road, full of difficulties but also full of hope. I would like not to forget, but to find dialogue again, and life.

S. Fatone

Sante Fatone was tried for terrorist activities and the re-establishment of an armed group with its headquarters in Milan and operating in Lombardy and Veneto under various names (Armed Proletariat for Communism, Communist Units for the Proletarian War, Communist Squads of the Proletariat Army and Armed Workers Squads). Sentenced to 25 years imprisonment in 1981 for the murder of Torregiani. Went into hiding while awaiting trial.

In August 1981, his parents Ciro Fatone and Rosa Scarano wrote a letter to their son, which was then published in various newspapers, asking him to return home. They stated that their lives had been threatened by the Red Brigades and that their son was not a terrorist.

On 15th June 1984 a Carabinieri patrol car stopped a car with Sante Fatone on board and he was wounded though he recovered in a few months. In 1985 the 2nd Court of Appeal in Milan sentenced him to nine years' imprisonment during the trial of the "Armed Proletariat for Communism" (a group similar to "Autonomia Operaia", founded in 1977). On 20th May 1985 he benefitted from a judicial pardon and is presently considered as one of the "superpentiti" – the repentant ".big-name" ex- terrorists. From his confessions investigators have extracted useful evidence which has shed light on certain serious episodes from the time of the "red terror". Thanks to evidence given by other ex-terrorists the courts have declared that some of the accused, because of their young age, were incapable of exercising any critical faculty upon the orders they received, and that they therefore acted without reflecting.

Mario Ferrandi

First Encounter

In my introduction I have spoken at length about Mario Ferrandi. What I would add here is that I continued to visit him in the various prisons where he was sent after extradition from London. When I visited him in prison at Piacenza I was shocked to see him so thin, like a skeleton. I don't know if he was on hunger strike at that time, but he appeared in front of me looking white, thin, full of suffering and disillusionment; I believe that he was going through a very difficult period in his life. It was as if he had had a breakdown perhaps due to his physical circumstances or some internal change. But then he recovered.

Letters

London, 8th July 1981

Dear Carmy,

By the time you've read this, I think I'll already be in Italy. In fact they've turned down my request to appeal, I knew they would, so it doesn't really matter. I could have let things drag on for another month or two but it would have been a waste of time. Anyway, if I want the Lord's mercy I've got to earn it and I can't sit here lazing around when people are getting slaughtered in Italy.

In these almost two years of exile I've worked out too many things to want to keep them to myself. And because I've made such serious mistakes so often, I consider it my duty to put things right, and try to light that same little spark of hope which lit up in me, inside my friends who are still lost in the mists of hate. What's more, I can tell you sincerely that being in prison doesn't bother me at all, I've found the peace here I've been looking for for years, I don't need to keep looking over my shoulder every hour, every minute; I've got nothing and nobody to be afraid of any more, and, paradoxically, I'm free, do you know what I mean? The worst is over, finished, cancelled, I'm not interested in it any more; now there's the future: concrete solutions for concrete problems – hey, you promised to visit me in Italy and I'm counting on it, you know – as soon as they've allocated me to a prison in Italy, I'll write and tell you where I am and if I like it. I'd like you to meet a whole lot of my friends too, but it depends where they send me.

Do you know I've still got a subscription to "Italia Missionaria" in Milan, the magazine of the Papal Agency for Foreign Missions? I've promised the Lord that if I can swing it, I'm going to put my sword to the service of some mission in Africa. I speak English, don't I? I can drive, too; I can do a whole lot of things, and what I don't know how to do I can learn. If I can't swing it, I'll think of something else.

News: Claudia wrote to me. My friends (or rather ex-friends) want me to change lawyers. My friend Giuseppe is desperate because he's getting an arrest warrant every week: I must go to the rescue. Pray for me because I have to face all of them and on my own too (OK, the Lord will be there but somehow I don't think he's about to show himself). There's one hell of a job to be done, what with all the various ex-terrorists and political prisoners in Italy. I'm going to have a go at studying the situation over there, and then I'll send you a detailed report on what I think needs doing. I've got a lot of ideas, but I have to check them out first. The fundamental thing right now is bringing them hope, do you see? Everything else, and how we'll do it, we can think about later. Listen, I don't know what else to tell you right now, so I'll just send you my love, and hope to see you again. Ciao.

Mario

Lodi, July 1981

85

Dear Carmelo,

Here I am, they've sent me to Lodi prison, near Milan. Imagine, we've got TV, wine, cookers, we can even order cakes from the local patisserie, we are four to a cell and seven political dissociates out of about sixty prisoners. They've sent me here because it seems that people in my position who get put in big prisons run the risk of either getting beaten up or as they like to say becoming "re-absorbed" and ending up playing at soldiers in this stupid war all over again. Quite apart from the initial jolt, the first weeks here were a disaster: I wasn't really used to being with other people any more, I started talking to myself and did all kinds of naughty things in my cell. Then I got used to it again and now I'm coping fine. The situation with my trial is worse than expected.

My only consolation is that the government looks certain to pass some new laws designed, it seems, to allow clemency for people who abandon the armed struggle. We'll see. Ah, I got your cigarettes just the moment before I was transferred, in fact I smoked them on the plane. I've been treated very well by everyone and my mum seemed fine too.

I can tell you right away that God is even more unpopular here than in the English prisons, but you can still find him here and there, even if hate, rancour, and the determination to do evil is the norm and everyone's dreaming of getting out so they can start doing what they did before all over again.

Listen, if you see my lawyer say hello to him from me. OK Carmy, must say goodbye now because it's lights out time. All my love, and hope to hear from you soon. Ciao.

Mario

Alessandria, January 1982

Ciao Carmelo,

It's 1982! I hope you're well as usual. I'm at Alessandria now with my friend Crippa and another ten or so of my old friends – all political prisoners.

I meant to tell you that this year for the first time we had

Mass at Christmas, we were the choir and a friend played the piano, with a good feast afterwards.

I really don't know if and when I'll be getting out, if and when I'll be able to go back over there; I could be out in a month, or a year, or never, I don't know. We don't even know under what laws they're going to consider our cases and judge us because they haven't made them yet.

Happy new year, and onward to new adventures.

Mario

Alessandria, April 1982

Hi Carmelo,

I'm sending you a copy of the local paper in Alessandria with some of our letters in it.

I'm quite well, there's a good chance of me getting out sooner or later and we've started a real revolution in this prison. At Easter we had Mass inside the wing with our relatives. They've let us have a colour TV. We've got a piano, a fishtank, an allotment, and we've started up our own newspaper. One of our friends was let out and he came to London. I gave him your address at the Italian church. You weren't there but they gave him some addresses and so he found a job and a house. He's written to say that he's still there, working in a "Spaghetti House". He's living in a boarding house run by Italians and he's just fine. My mum is well. Thanks for the postcards. Love.

Mario

P.S. Say hello to Addezio if you see him. Ciao.

Alessandria, September 1982

Ciao Carmelo,

Listen, there are some things which I didn't have time to tell you when we last met because I was so bowled over at actually seeing you in front of me. The first thing was that I'm amazed how when you create a dialogue with people instead of confrontation, all kinds of doors suddenly start opening up for you.

Second, that loving people is hard, hard, hard, but you have to keep on trying.

Next: all you really have to do is let yourself go and follow the signs that are there, and suddenly your next move appears in front of you. And consequently you feel the thrill of being part of a plan.

Since I came here everything seems to have magically sprung into life, everything we need or want appears by itself, exactly when we need it most.

Only I can't tell this to everyone, otherwise they'll all think I'm a looney, I just keep on doing it and that's that.

I'll send you the newspaper, which speaks for itself. In a month from now I've decided to ask the authorities to let me go free because somebody's got to set up some kind of shelter abroad for this band of wretches which is what we are which to tell the truth was what I was already doing in London when I was out. The first thing to do is to either convince or force, I'm not sure yet, the powers that be, damn them, trust us; but I feel I've got to try, to free us to free others. Love has to be organised like guerilla warfare. Bye.

Mario

Piacenza, January 1983

Dear Carmelino,

How are you? I'm on the point of becoming a Franciscan monk! No, I'm joking; but they've transferred me and my friend Giuseppe to Piacenza where even though we are worse off than in Alessandria, we've found a load of things we needed. Together with the chaplain we're organising a massive alms-begging session so we can try and set up a place where prisoners, including us, can go to find work outside.

From the moment I chose to try the way of faith, the whole of my life as well as the lives of the people I care about, have changed. At times I'm happy; so many incredible things are happening: MPs have visited me, newspapers are asking for my life story. We are working towards a humanitarian solution for political prisoners, we're talking about using social work instead of jail. I met a millionaire who wants to set up a fund to help us. Sometimes I dream about sorting out the whole of this business of political prisoners and then chucking up everything and coming over to help you with a little army of brothers.

I always think of you as the one who brought the light into my senseless life and I will always love you for it.

Unfortunately at Alessandria I wasn't able to say goodbye to the friends or those brothers. They keep us separated from other prisoners for security reasons. The bishop of Piacenza is coming soon to celebrate Mass in our wing; he came to bless us this Christmas. He looked like a small Pope. All my love.

Mario

Piacenza, April 1983

Listen, Carmelo, I have decided to fight in order to bring me and my friends back towards life, and the road I've chosen is that of non-violence.

I don't believe in silence or submission, and discovering Christianity showed me the way towards light, hope and revelation; it was a stage on a path which I clearly see and feel, for me to follow, it was a plan, do you see?

I walk along this road following the signs which the Lord sets up along it for me, often ignoring other people's opinions. I don't look for the tools, I collect them along the way, because when I need them, they turn up.

I walk amongst the chaos, following an order which is invisible to everyone else. Christ has already sacrificed himself so that our lives would not be a Calvary, but a battle against evil which has already been won by obedience to the law of love. He calls us and we, freely, obey.

I am a miserable sinner who has chosen to redeem himself by working for a political solution for political prisoners who have chosen to become normal citizens once again, and that is extremely important. No one will change my mind. I'll be a worker for peace and I will see God. I pray for this. I ask God for energy and God gives it to me; it's wonderful, do you understand?

Don't worry about me. I am in His hands. I feel, I know, that everything is going to be OK. All my love to you.

Mario

P.S. Giuseppe says hello.

Piacenza, 12th August 1983

Hi Carmelino,

How are things over there? Did you come to Italy? What are the Italian prisoners up to? I'm just starting my trial here.

I've fallen in love. Faith is my only salvation. At times it seems as if I am about to lose it, I am on the verge of despair, and suddenly a light appears. Everything I thought before is starting to work. I am tormented by my longing to get out of here, but then I try to be sensible, and try to love.

Sometimes I can't see what's good straight away, but I always get there in the end. I'm going to make it! Lots of love.

Mario

Piacenza, 25th August 1983

Hi Carmelino,

It's Mario. Listen, it's late at night and I'm keeping vigil, it's August 25th. I want to tell you, there have been nasty moments and nice moments and there'll be more of both, but the hope and faith you have given me back have never let me down and I am grateful to you. My life is hard but it has a meaning, a light to lead me on. I'll never turn back on this path, God's path, and just thinking about it makes me forget the difficulties and gives me the energy to keep going. May God protect you and help you to snatch other lives from despair. All my love and best wishes to you. Ciao.

Mario

Milan, March 1986

Dear Carmelo,

Great is the disorder beneath the heavens, so things are looking very promising. The way towards reconciliation is progressing apace, and the things I have to tell you are so many and varied that I'll have to wait until we see each other.

You didn't tell me that Channel 5 asked you to come to Rome!

I am up to my ears in work. Tonight I'm having dinner with Balducci, someone else the Lord has brought back into His gang – you'll definitely meet him soon. All my love, from Mara too, and Valerio (who is quite a little man already!). Ciao.

Mario

Milan, 19th June 1987

Ciao Carmelo,

How are you? I got your postcard from Poland. What's the news over there? I hoped to see you. Things are going so so.

Mara and Valerio are fine and my job too, even if all the nasty little intrigues often cause us setbacks and difficulties; they're things which I am sure you know about better than I do myself.

I am developing a passion for the history of the early Christians, reading archaeological magazines and various publications about excavations of the catacombs: you can really see how those communities despite their poverty and illness really were a truthful answer to man's needs. I think you should come here to Milan. This is where we should start, but I don't have enough strength or faith; I'm too selfish and cowardly. And lazy.

You've got to come here and start a community, we should get a parish and be holy terrors. All my love.

Mario

Mario Ferrandi, born in Milan on 12th December 1955. Student of philosophy at Milan University. Joined the armed struggle in 1973, after the "Workers' Power" movement, of which he was a member, had been disbanded, he joined the "Red" Movement and then in 1977 the "Front Line". In 1978 he played a part in the campaign against drug pushers following which he was condemned for murder. In October 1979 he went into hiding in London. In October 1980 he was arrested and in August 1981 was extradited to Italy. He was detained in the prison at Lodi until October of the same year. From November 1981 until December 1982 he was imprisoned in Alessandria and then transferred to Piacenza. In October 1983 he was sentenced to one and a half years' detention following the trial for the murder of the journalist Walter Tobagi. In October 1984 he was sentenced to six years' imprisonment at the "Front Line" trial. In November of the same year he was provisionally freed. In August 1985 he agreed to go on trial for political crimes (membership of an armed gang, etc.) and in September 1986 was taken into custody again and put under house arrest. He is still under house arrest today, with permission to do community work under the supervision of the Don Calabria drug rehabilitation project. Whilst imprisoned in Alessandria, Ferrandi published a paper called, "Breaking the Rules of this Absurd Game" in which he wrote, "a violent act is also a desperate cry for help. A full, blind, redeeming confession is another aspect of the same impulse. What I have observed in myself is that resolving dichotomies of this kind inevitably leads one towards the sacred."

Angelo Izzo

I only knew Angelo Izzo through what had been said and written about him. They had labelled him a "monster". Then someone spoke to me about him, and asked me to go and see him. I didn't even know which prison he was in.

The first time I went to Paliano prison, a few years ago, I well remember that he was the first person to come to meet me when I got through all the prison gates. I remember the scene. Angelo Izzo on one side, Valerio Morucci a bit further forward, then Antonio Savasta, Faranda and others. Angelo Izzo came towards me, and we went to talk on our own. We talked for over an hour. I was almost afraid when I found myself in front of him but at the same time I could hardly believe that this was the same Angelo Izzo I had heard people talking about.

I saw that he had no difficulty in opening his heart to me. He was the first to speak and it was like a flood, a torrent of experiences. I saw that he knew what people thought about him and the opinion society had of him. Confronted with this situation I told him, "Christ loves you for what you are with all the dross of your past and he proves this to you on the Cross. There is a chance for you to live a new life, you can be reborn despite everything that society thinks about you, despite the fact that it wants you shut out." I remember that he seemed to find it hard to understand and accept such a message. Then I noticed that his eyes were full of tears.

Paliano, 22nd August 1987

Dearest Carmelo,

I'm taking advantage of an old friend in prison in London to write to you, and to thank you for the lovely postcards you sent me from London and Formosa. Everything is okay here, I'm surviving, I hope to get out soon and I'm longing to see you again.

I was given permission to go home for a few hours for my sister's wedding, it was great, as you can imagine. Let's hope they make up their minds to let me out, after 12 years inside these walls, eight of which in maximum security prisons, I reckon it's about time! I am a totally different person to what I was at the time I committed the things I ended up inside for. Excuse the outburst. Show up soon. I send you all my brotherly love.

Angelo

Paliano, 22nd October 1987

My dear Carmelo,

I received your letters and I am answering them immediately. I hope to write to you soon and tell you a bit about my state of mind and the changes which it has pleased God to make in me, helping me out of the tunnel of my futile past. I was very interested to hear about your trip and it was really nice to hear that you're so happy.

Things are pretty much the same here, life's a bit hard mainly because, once someone stops wanting to do any harm any more, prison becomes a bit like pointless cruelty. Plus no matter how hard I try to pick myself up, no matter how much I hope and dream of getting my life together again, the prospects are bleak, and it gets worse more and more all the time, dammit. I came in here when I was 19 and now I'm thirty-two and it looks like they want to keep me here until I'm an old man. Forget it; I don't want to depress you with my laments.

Write soon. All my love to you.

Angelo

My dearest Carmelo,
I received your letter yesterday and I'm answering straight
away. Unfortunately I am in the process of being transferred. I would be very happy if you could come and visit
me.
As I told you before, I want to tell you a bit about me
and my life.
I was born in an upper-middle class bourgeois family,
a very close family which always provided everything,
affection too. But ever since I was a teenager I've always
possessed a longing for rebellion and intolerance towards
having a so-called "normal life". When I was only 14 I
began to get involved in extremist right-wing politics –
groups like the "National Vanguard" (Avanguardia Nazio-
nale) and later with the "People's Struggle" (Lotta di Popolo).
It was an almost casual decision because I wasn't really
interested in ideology or politics, although I did think I
could resolve my existential problems with violence. While
I was still a teenager I was in trouble more than once for
fighting and armed assault. I was also involved in attempts
to blow up houses, cars and offices belonging to leftist
militants and their parties. And then, gradually, together
with some of my "comrades", friends I had practically
grown up with, we formed a gang which hovered between
political and common delinquency. We were a small, very
harmonious group, seeing that we had known each other
since childhood, we all lived nearby, our families were
friends and we had been friends at school, and all these
things turned us into a closed and paranoid unit which
thought it was "at war" with the world! We were totally
convinced that we were a group of mercenaries in enemy
territory. And gradually we slipped into a spiral of ever
increasing violence!
Between the age of 18 until my arrest at the age of 21
my life was a series of robberies in banks and jewellers,
rapes, arms and drug trafficking. We always carried guns
and by now I was a prisoner in a trap which I had set
myself. Until the murder. A horrible murder which was

almost without motive and was the reason for my arrest and sentence of life imprisonment.

I lived out my first years in prison like a continuation of my previous life. I made friends with prisoners belonging to the "revolutionary right", I tried to escape with a gun in my hand, I often got into fights between rival prison gangs. And because of my bad behaviour I was sent to a maximum security prison for eight years where I was put under a very strict regime. But in solitary confinement I came into contact with the pain and suffering of other human beings, I had a profound change of heart about my life and my actions. I realised how horrible violence committed by man against man is, the violence of injustice, and the oppression of one man by another. I realised that I was throwing away my life by doing harm. And slowly my life changed. Among other things, by setting out on a journey of "repentance" and attempting to set right the damage I had done. This is the reason why I collaborated with the Law. I did not get nor did I ask for any material benefit for doing this.

I find it difficult talking about a period of light in the darkness of my life. I would say that when I decided to tear off this tight-fitting suit, the "hard man's" suit, the suit of violence, it was very difficult, because it's not easy to deny your past: it was, after all, a comfortable suit. Specially when you bear in mind that my life had already been "marked", there was no room for turning back. You see, faith helped me then; God gave me strength and prevented me from falling into despair.

Ciao, Carmelo, I hope to see you again and if you want we can talk some more about it. Love.

Angelo Izzo

Livio Lai

I met Livio Lai at Rome's Rebibbia Prison along with Franc-eschini, Gidoni, Cavallina and others. He seemed an intelligent, cultured and well-educated person. He was interested in setting up amateur dramatics in the prison and was also involved in trying to promote the process of reconciliation started by the "area omogenea", or "united group", where both right and left wing terrorists had come together.

Letters

Rome, 11th April 1987

My dear Carmelo,

I found your package and some of your postcards on a chair, and it makes me smile to think of getting in touch with you again. A long time has passed since last September. Time in prison is very strange. It's meaningless. Being a prisoner means being suspended in a time vacuum. So don't be surprised at the delay. As far as I am concerned it's nothing; but you know all about that, you've been "in" prisons longer than I have. I'm only aware of periods of time through what happens outside: but in spirit, I live outside. The constant waiting and the constant "false" news. New developments which look as if they're going to make my/our dreams become reality: they disappear and then they come back again. Trying to work out the things that are important, so they can "immunize" me against this see-saw of hopes. I am going through a stage when everything seems so... superfluous. I don't think it's resignation or lack of willpower, it's more like a kind of trance where I'm completely impervious about what fate has in store for me. I'm almost like a parcel in the post: except that I am aware of my state. It's not indifference either, because that implies an acceptance / rejection relationship with the situation. Maybe it's acceptance of myself, of my condition.

Starting right here, right now, without yearning for some far-off paradise (freedom) desperately trying to understand those powerful mechanisms of defence/attack that the human mind contrives – the selfish ego as its dominant principle – to build a barrier of identity where you can know yourself again and be known again by others. And so to survive. But why always deceive yourself and others? Maybe that's exactly how conflicts between men are born: the will to impose oneself in order to survive, the selfishness of life, the fear of looking too hard at oneself. But what would mankind be without conflict? Life is a continual encounter/clash too, in a paradoxical sequence of contradictions, futilities and joys. Which obliges me to go back to where I started. No answers, no joys.

Everything begins again, everything ends. An ostensible ending, comforted solely by a self-appropriation of the mirage. Happy Easter to you, brother, and all my friends up there in the North.

A fond farewell.

Livio

Rome, 14 March 1988

My dear Carmelo,

I am sending you a synopsis of my life, so you can have a wider and clearer picture of me and my past and, why not, of my present/future.

I am 34 years old, I was born in Trieste and I've been in prison since 1982, since the 21st of April of that year to be exact. They arrested me as I was trying to run away from a cottage near Treviso with a pistol and a false police ID in my bag. I was wanted for belonging to the right-wing Armed Revolutionary Squads, the specific charges being murder, membership of an armed gang and criminal association to cause subversion, armed robbery and other crimes.

I had been on the run abroad (in Lebanon), in hiding since 1980. I received total sentences of more than 40 years imprisonment. During two trials I benefited from the law of political dissociation, with irrevocable sentences. An appeal hearing for the third trial still has to take place.

After three years inside I joined up with the "united group for political dissociation from terrorism" at Rebibbia Prison, where I am in close touch with left-wing terrorists and right-wing extremists.

I am partner in a cooperative for cultural and agricultural production, founded here in prison by both common and political prisoners. My main interest is in the theatre, and I have been assistant producer in several productions.

I am about to take a degree in law and my thesis is, of course, on prison.

My future was decided on a beach in the summer of 1975, one of the many which line the Riviera of Trieste. We were a group of young people like any others, but with a special dedication to politics. Having experienced only secondhand what had occurred in the preceding years, much too engrossed in my cocoon of sport, study and having fun, I suddenly found myself in the whirlwind of politics. But my first approach was fundamentally human: a profound relationship of friendship won me over, a sense of togetherness I'd never known before, a continuous vitality, a lack of concern for one's own interests, a continual atmosphere of fun and enthusiasm. I only became "politicized" later, but I felt as if I was simply discovering things I had always had inside me. Seemingly new, but internally already present.

This period lasted only a shortwhile: then riots, ambushes, picket lines and street fighting started to characterise my life. I recognised myself in all this now, the tiny simulation of a tiny war, which let me experience all those behavioural characteristics which I thought of as belonging to the neo-fascist and to him alone: courage, self-denial, sacrifice, loyalty, sense of duty, dedication. Everyone was anti-fascist, from the cultural world to the media, from the ordinary people to the judiciary. A continual sense of being "outside" and "against". Always outcast, rejected, ghettoized. And this feeling of being excluded was to prove decisive.

So it's easy, considering the climate of the 70's, to see how the consequences of such a culture should be intolerance, hatred and violence.

This was the basis for my involvement in politics, the initial push which catapulted me into it, during the second half of the 70's, and which in fact had little to do with politics in the strict sense of the word but rather more with sentimental fantasies about politics.

Communism was our principal enemy, if not the only one; my party adopted it unquestioningly, and charged towards it, almost as if to divert attention from other more concrete realities of exploitation and power. How is it possible for two kids of the same age, from the same school, the same class, to arrive at such violent opposition? The certainty of possessing the truth on the one side, and the conviction that the enemy represented all the "evil" in the world, on the other. I never asked myself that question then. I was too busy pursuing and being pursued, running around in a garden where all the political powers calmly sat, looking cynically on without knowing who was the pursued and who the pursuer. People had to die before we could finally escape from that illusion of opposite extremisms.

In Trieste we were living through pretty significant times and one factor which was very much in our favour played its part in the continuous battle of wearing down the opposite political faction: the ceding of the so-called "zone B" to Yugoslavia, following the Treaty of Osimo.

We, the right-wing student activists of the Fronte della Gioventù, the Youth Front, were especially involved in the hard-hitting campaign which was launched as a consequence – in the schools and in various parts of the city, and which induced significant numbers of people to protest in the streets and which ended in clashes with the police. A spontaneous gathering that we could infiltrate and steer and guide into an organised force. It was the same in the schools, where sit-ins, marches and processions were directly instigated by the Youth Front activists, thus giving us a clear political superiority and putting us on the lists of bona fide parties within the schools. The predominance of young left-wingers had been broken, not least because the battle for "an Italian Trieste" had thrown them into confusion, so much so that our members used to mix with the marches that they were unable to control.

But I tended to face these struggles in a somewhat disenchanted frame of mind. It was 78-79 and the Italian flag and nationalism were just a way of reaching an objective which as far as I was concerned was becoming more and more real and obvious all the time: the establishment, the forces of law and order, the system. The exaltation and the joy of the fight, the smell of the molotovs, the perfume of the teargas, the charges, the retreats, the cobblestones we threw: the perception of the enemy's immediate presence. But for the first time, being consciously on the side of the people too, no longer outsiders but their direct and accepted representatives in the common struggle. This influenced me enormously, because it enabled me to realise, even if only on the basis of an abstract and sentimental notion, my wish to take an active role in society, which had been born during the events of 1977.

So next there were the protests against the rising cost of living: we organised second-hand school book markets, distributed bread at a fixed low price (we called it the "political price"), and opened cut-price food stores. Then there were the campaigns against the inefficiency of public transport, against the housing shortage, founding new movements of unemployed workers or ecology groups. But these briefly-described attempts to get out of the ghetto were still isolated and disorganised episodes due to their improvisation and lack of planning and proper research and social and cultural hinterland; however seen as a whole they demonstrate the existence of groups and people who were looking for their own specific identity, more closely in line with their requirements.

Even the gut level anti-communism, almost the only motive behind most day-to-day right-wing activity, was brought into question. The views of the extreme left-wing were looked at with a certain interest, we were all involved in the expulsion of Luciano Lama, the leader of the left-wing union, from the university, in the deaths of our comrades killed by the police, in the activities of the armed groups. The idea of urban guerillas was the common ground in our imaginations; their fantasy, spirituality and existentialism seemed to destroy or at least question the rigidity and immutability of the Marxist-Leninist myths. You can be comrades without putting on Brezhnev's funeral face, or without having assemblies as icy cold and inscrutable as a meeting of the Politburo. Nobody was talking about political alliance – such a thing could not be mooted – but you could admire the evolution of the left and begin to see it in a different light, you could agree with them in a whole lot of ways. A desire to understand and to be understood. Even if the absolutisation of our ideas made us think that it was them who resembled us, and we saw reflected in them our own characteristics and peculiarities (they were right-wing comrades gone astray!). So some meetings were organized, we tried to talk, to get closer to them, understand them, be open with them. We gave interviews to local left-wing newspapers: behind the communist, behind the neo-fascist, unimaginable human and political realities were being discovered. So the use of violence became gradually more general albeit at the theoretical acceptance or inevitable necessity level and the Armed Revolutionary Squads were simply the most extreme practical manifestation of this. There were people who were opposed to this giddy escalation, but they brought about deceleration rather than a total stoppage of the process, dragged along by this atmosphere of totalisation which our generation was breathing, taking part in debates on violence in general, on the right to judge others, on the deeper significance of actions, on general political theory, on behavioural procedures.

But taking the next step, towards increased politicization, got smashed against the classic wall of the superficiality of slogans, passwords.

The attempt to achieve environment-conscious autoresponsibilization failed, and the fact of indiscriminate impact with totally different realities, albeit ideologically similar, watered down the F.U.A.N, our University-based organisation, and it lost its ability to function as an information centre. The division was not only about the legality or otherwise of armed struggle but also about various individuals' different perceptions of how to relate to society. It was a relationship based on isolation, violence, reformism, political or nonpolitical indifference. But everyone made the same basic error; the arrogance of believing you were the only ones to have chosen the right path and that this legitimised all your actions. So by 1979 there were some people who went into hiding, some who carried out isolated armed attacks, some who used arms for personal reasons, some who retired into private life, some who were laying down the foundations for a future life, even by occasionally helping anyone who needed it and had maintained strong ties of friendship with them, and some people who tried to transfer the experience of community living outside the urban chaos.

A communal experience was over, a new phase was beginning, for many of us a more crude, more violent and more tragic one.

Three months of being on the run in Rome gave me the chance of getting to know the circuit really well and to forge links which are still strong, beyond politics.

In Rome I was living in a situation with a much higher level of dispute with the left, there was a generalised mass lawlessness, day-by-day activities on the fringe of legality: transgression was the permanent symbol. Everything that was anti (morality, customs, the state) was taken up as a revolutionary ideal. Weapons just stand for the exasperation of these concepts, the ultimate expression of "anti" feelings. Out of our first requirements of pure self-defence we began to identify policemen, the carabinieri, judges as more satisfactory targets for our purposes. They represented what we were existentially furthest away from (order, discipline, patriotism and the family), and so now we were inside an infinite chain of antagonism and never-ending repression. Amongst all the possible choices, the armed-conflictist was the most consistent with everything in my past. It was almost against my will the only choice I could have made.

For me it was the only consistent choice, even at the cost

of the inconceivable final sacrifice. The Lebanese experience had made the use of weapons an even more practical choice for me, with the arms training I had received there. So my return to Italy after some months in hiding in France and England was a logical consequence, which I felt as my political duty, to be a witness to the struggle, as a moral duty to outlive the comrades killed or imprisoned, be faithful to my own thinking and to myself and to continue practising and living my ideals to the utmost. And not going to join the others who were living in hiding in Italy seemed like betraying them.

My arrest marked the abrupt ending of the spiral of violence which we had thrown ourselves into. Once within it took only a few months for a critical and objective state of mind to emerge. It however seemed natural and immediate, since there was no severe trauma or fragmentation accompanying it, almost as though it were a direct consequence of what we had been before, outside.

Later, I also discovered what might have been one of the many possible reasons, together with my brother and some others who shared these moments of reflection. Within the concept and use of violence which starts as a mode of expression, a means of communication, neutral in its use, but which becomes a fundamental force in the transformation of the individual, modifying within the subject the parameters of his relationships with others. A continued or prolonged use of weapons, a psychological dependence on them withers interpersonal relationships by emptying them and stripping them of their greater worth, forcing one to forget the needs of others, the value of sentiments, the values of life, of man. Feelings of friendship, of group solidarity, can be exalted by "trench comradeship" but at the same time the pre-eminent reason for their existence is to be found in weapons.

From here to my joining the "United Group" at Rebibbia prison was a long road. An extremely painful and intimate process full of doubts, of imbalance, during which every perception of mistakes made was consciously internalised. Dissociation does not only appear to us as a superficial abandoning of logic and discrimination, a simple detachment from certain mental processes in order to comply with others of a different nature, an outward condemnation of ideological schemes that legalised the abrogation to oneself of the right to interfere with the destiny of another man. For me it certainly does not mean a refusal of my past self, a wish to forget the totalizing dimension in which I was immersed, a rejection of our simplistic and rigorous reading of reality. Neither was it an escape towards the future, an attempt to free myself from my responsibilities, a flight from what I was.

Dissociation takes on a value for me insofar as I attempted to understand more deeply the closed, intolerant behaviour which had characterised me and which not only has a political and physical objectivization but also a further likeness in the mental attitude of arrogance, excluding other values and other visions.

Thus I faced the discomfort of re-examining and dismantling all my past behaviour, discovering the deceits present within the conception of enmity, of the superficiality of judgements, of the sterility of violence, I was left with a sense of impotence, with the awareness that one cannot do anything to remedy the pain caused, and the pain suffered, to reconstruct the shattered lives of those I considered enemies and others whom I held dear. Perhaps it is impossible to create an awareness of all this, perhaps such a deep inner experience can only find expression in the way I am now trying to relate with people around me, through the continual practise of respect and acceptance of every nature and reality: it is the sensitivity that I intend to base all my future behaviour on, in whatever area of life it should be called for.

My arrival at the "United Group" in Rebibbia can be divided into three stages; the overcoming of the violence and the ideology and the central position it had taken in my life; the criticism of and detachment from a right-wing view of the world, almost the completion of a process which had started in 1977; the desire to do social work, almost as a form of reparation for the damage caused, especially in prison, which represents one of the most rejected and ghettoized sectors of society.

Distancing oneself from an ideology is a bit like knocking down a wall and finding yourself standing in front of an immense sea of grass. Ideologies become fixed in an absolute vision of the world and claim to offer unique and absolute answers to every social and human occurrence and phenomenon, insofar as they insert them into a precise and single plan. And often man, as I saw it, was in practice valued chiefly for his social function, deprived of his richness. A richness which makes me see him now as totally unique in his daily existence, which makes me see the immensity of existence and the infinite possibilities of life with equal dignity and value: here lies the basis of my change, a different feeling towards my fellow man, a different way of being, a different relationship with society.

And so it happened that all my ideas of counter-power and confrontation fell away and I started considering new hypotheses of dialogue and debate, of the understanding and openness needed to achieve collective and individual growth and maturity.

And this enables me now to live without difficulty with my comrades, who have experienced a similar process. And now we mimic ironically the characters we used to be. Once the ideological barriers have fallen, we look at our fellow man for what he is and from our comparisons with the past we realise how many phantoms there were in our minds, how concerned we used to be with our fear of the fascist or of the communist, and how tiny was the difference between landing on the shores of the right or the left. Both communists and fascists felt ghettoized and saw the enemy gathered on a single front, along with all the other political forces. And what I find most fascinating of all is the similarity of our mental processes; an ideology is the product and not the basis of intolerant thinking. The central core of it is the schematisms to which our brains are subject. Changing the referentials of "truth" is no use, it is better if we try to understand the source of incomprehension in our own minds.

And here my previous inclination of tending towards work within prisons can find its collective concretization since prisons are still an over-totalizing structure, the product of a culture based on the rejection of whatever is different, on the demonization of the deviant, on the painful expiation of guilt, but which today does nothing but produce and reproduce delinquency, impeding the tangible rehabilitation of the offender. And as I live out the reality of prison every day, this is the most serious deficiency I can see; the impossibility of communicating, the continuous sense of isolation, the suffocation of every personal initiative. The prison system should be structured around making the best use of the individual's abilities, his rehabilitation, until such time as he can feel he is an integral part of the community. His relationship with the outside world, with social and cultural workers, is therefore fundamental, so that society can come into the prison and the prison is no longer an island of isolation within our country.

With much affection.

Livio

Bruno Laronga

First Encounter

I first met Bruno Laronga two years ago in the prison at Bergamo along with Chicco Galmozzi and some others. It was a very moving meeting. Bruno really opened his heart to me, and had no difficulty in talking to me about his life and the trials too. He is very intelligent and highly-educated, capable of profound political and personal analysis. What struck me most about him was the way he managed to formulate political solutions for all the problems.

Letters

Bergamo, 1st May 1988

Dear Carmelo,

I would like to talk to you a little about myself and my life since the age of 6, when my parents and I "emigrated", as they say, to Sesto San Giovanni near Milan, from San Severo di Foggia in southern Italy, where I was born on 15th April 1953.

As a student, I took part in the first demonstrations of 1968 as a member of some of the extra-parliamentary organisations which then existed; I was sympathetic to the left-wing movement Lotta Continua (Continuous Struggle), and like many others – who subsequently joined Prima Linea, the Front Line – we were very critical of the decision made by that group, in the 1975 elections, to back the Italian Communist Party for government (these were local government elections).

Between this crisis-point and the dissolution of Lotta Continua I decided to join in the debate which was taking place within the movement on the question of the use of violence, the debate which later brought the various armed

108

groups into being (except the Red Brigades which had been formed earlier).

In 1976 we were already a completely independent armed group confederated under the name Prima Linea, with representatives in various cities: Milan, Turin, Florence, Rome and Naples. I was one of the founders of the group.

In May 1977 I moved to Turin where there was already an active cell. At the end of that year, more than 300 people either belonged to our group or were sympathisers: it certainly wasn't the clandestine armed struggle promoted by the Red Brigades: we were much more closely allied to those popular protest movements which had sparked off the demonstrations in Bologna than to the groups which carried out the kidnapping and murder of Aldo Moro (the Italian Prime Minister) and the killing of his police escort.

Nevertheless our politico-military action in Turin was certainly not mere propaganda: we also carried out political homicide, various leading figures were knee-capped including government department heads, and professional men who met with particular criticism (psychiatrists who beat their patients, gynecologists who charged exorbitantly for abortions etc.).

The main emphasis of our actions was either the desire to do justice or else they were directed at the promotion of proletarian combat (as we called it...), these actions were then delegated to the armed groups present in the area who had more specific functions.

Our conception of the avant-garde armed struggle, at least in intention, depended on a dialectic process taking place between us, the central organisation, and the movement; we aimed to arm ourselves from the grass roots level upwards, starting with the specific needs of the proletariat within the cities; the organisation was basically conceived as a service to and a means of self-defence for the movement.

The kidnapping and the murder of Aldo Moro, dictated by a centralised and Leninist idea of the role of the armed organisation, of the party which elected itself as the conscience and the directing body of the whole "class", represented a point of no return for all the armed organisations, for the movements themselves and for the various scattered groups over which we wished to exercise control. This concept of ours, based on the growth of military and armed activity in the region, contrasted with the Red Brigades' idea of an "apparatus" of State against State, which was totally foreign to us.

So Moro's kidnapping represented a forced development as regards the growth pattern of the movement, because the reaction it unleashed within the State compelled each one of us to readjust to the level which the conflict had now reached. The Moro operation took its place in the ideological self-view of this armed movement as a demand for the vertical organisation of the struggle, and it must also be said that many of us were not immune from this either: the geometrical power of the kidnapping became a by-now-unattainable but constantly striven-for level of confrontation, for which most people were unprepared. This also meant abandoning our jobs and our physical presence within our regions of origin. Nor should it remain unsaid that the reaction of the State subsequently compelled many of us to resort to clandestinity, for which we were unprepared.

The price of this rush forward was our uprooting, marked by a split between the movements and its vanguards. The former was impotent, delegating more and more, while the latter became more and more specialised and ferocious, as if they were fighting a private war against the State.

Under these circumstances collapse in the face of arrest was entirely predictable, and the so-called phenomenon of "repentance" revealed the extreme weakness of the hitherto very mysterious armed organisations: the repentant "big name" Red Brigade terrorists Peci and Sandalo alone caused the arrest of more than 400 people: a sure sign that everybody knew everything!

I was arrested on the 8th May 1980 in via Lorenteggio in Milan together with my wife Silveria, Pino Polo and Filiberto Cane. During eight years of imprisonment I have been through all the top-security prisons in Italy, and in many different courts, facing charges in Milan, Turin, Naples, Sassari, Rome, Florence... all pretty heavy ones too.

The trials themselves were an opportunity for meetings and discussions among ourselves, with comrades we hadn't seen for years and new recruits, and our decisions to dissolve the group and to disassociate from it matured right there, conscious as we were of the impracticability and erroneousness of our past decisions: in fact, it wasn't so much our continuity that was in discussion but the very existence of the movement, the reality for which and in which to fight. A movement which, in those very years, was to receive its most dramatic defeats among the workers at the Fiat plant and in the streets of towns all over the country. We were not driven so much by the vision of an ideology as by the vision of a movement, which certainly made it easier for us to understand our mistakes: not just those mistakes that history made clear to us, but also those that deep within us spoke of the presumption of passing judgement on our own and others' lives and deaths. It's a heavy burden of responsibility which it is still difficult to live with.

Today, as you well know, dear Carmelo, I am labouring back up the slope towards normal life: my son was born two months ago, I work in a youth centre as a supplementary teacher... but there are still many years to be spent in prison before I have my freedom. My present sentence is 22 years 6 months but I am still under a suspended life sentence.

Yours affectionately,
Bruno

Bergamo, 1st May 1988

Dear Carmelo,

The recent killing of Senator Ruffilli by the Communist Combatant Party Red Brigade, quite apart from my human dismay at the gesture, sharpened by having myself once played a role in similar dramas, gives rise to several points for reflection.

The first myth which must be destroyed is that of the existence of some wise old "Big Boss", in contact with secret destabilisation cells (the secret services or the P2 Lodge). This theory runs the risk of resurrecting that old theory which was especially dear to several sectors of the Italian Communist Party in the seventies who saw the armed groups as mercenaries and the knowing or unknowing paid agent provocateurs of revolution; or else that theory of nondenominational-Republican extraction which states that violence "is always and only fascist". Accompanying this vision of the new terrorism are the eternal questions, even when there's really nothing more to be asked, about the Moro affair. Even if some obscure aspects of this episode remain, for example about the behaviour of the secret services contaminated by the P2 at the time, it should really teach us that these aspects cannot overshadow a truth about Italian terrorism which emerged in the courts: that it is absolutely independent from central government and its apparatus, and its political and cultural origins derive from an environment which is obviously of the extreme left. Such theories of terrorism, besides being false on a historical level, are also dangerous at a political level because by failing to understand the phenomenon they risk bringing about the development of inadequate counter-measures. Basing one's analysis of terrorism rather on its autonomous and autochthonous nature helps one to understand not just past history but also a part at least of the present mechanisms.

I simply wish to recall the interpretations of the phenomenon which have been made in past years; and not only the actions of the armed organisations but even the demands and actions of certain mass movements were relegated by political parties, mainly the left-wing ones, to being defined as "irrational", mere youthful discontent, provocation, by a process of the quashing of every politico-cultural interpretation of the phenomenon. This kind of interpretation of events even produced its own specific semantics, speaking of "gangism", "teenageism" and similar epithets.

As a result, in my opinion, we find ourselves faced with a self-contained phenomenon, with a distorted vision of the national political horizon as its premise. Above all the recent case of the document claiming responsibility for the killing of Ruffilli seems to go beyond that internationalist or "euro-terrorist" phase which had characterised the residual fragments of the armed struggle. Their present claim is that they wish to have an influence on specific areas of Italian political life, such as institutional reform, entering as a permanent intermediary on the political scene. If, at one time, an attempt to mobilise the classes was joined to their pursuit of destabilisation and of armed conflict with the State, nowadays the sights of this so-called "Fighting Communist Party" (Partito Comunista Combattente) are above all set on parliament, whose language it has even begun to adopt.

So it would appear that their political action is moving along the lines of a very long drawn-out conflict and that the military actions serve to mark their presence in the national political framework. Perhaps they hope to "benefit" from these actions in some future political set-up whose nature is completely unknown. This is the basic distinction between the old and the new terrorism. The first armed struggle claimed to be the dialectical core of the mass struggle; this second one acts with the principle of institutional destabilisation in mind, and the construction of a political party for the revolution to come. So, unfortunately, one cannot fail to recognise a politicization which is anything but residual in this "Fighting Communist Party", and we must therefore be prepared to live with what has by now become a permanent feature of our political life.

Defining the new Red Brigades as merely crazy fragments is more like whistling in the dark than a hypothesis based on real facts. In fact they must have a base in society however limited; an area of recruitment however select; a place where they can take the pulse of political activity, however well-hidden... yet even so I maintain that this terrorist phenomenon must be approached calmly. In fact the seduction of revolution has lost a great deal of its fascination and plausibility; social conflictuality has become depoliticised; the international context itself is experiencing a new era of detente; and so conditions do not appear to be right for a resumption of the armed struggle like the one we saw explode in the Seventies. If anything, the future risk is a different, and social one: in the face of the insurgence of new transformational movements, these new Red Brigades might have to become not so much a pole of political reference as an incitement to the fascination of violence.

If it is unarguable that at the root of the dramatic events of the Seventies there lay an inadequacy on the part of the political powers to accept demands for the emancipation and the transformation of various sectors of society, then the consequence of such shortcomings could be of use in preventing new social demands becoming linked to terrorist ideas. It is obvious that "dissociation" has weighed heavily on the political delegitimisation of the armed struggle by emptying it from within of all its substance and motivation. But it is also clear that the politicians' inability to face up to their own errors, this unpreparedness, this detachment from the needs of the country, is a serious handicap against any effective campaign against present-day terrorism. What's more, if we take this endemicity for granted, as unfortunately we must, then really facing up to the problems of reforms tending to broadening democratic participation in political activity would facilitate a gradual elimination of the temptations of violence and the creation of a buffer zone around those who wish to imitate the events of the terrorist decades.

Even now, we hear rhetoric about the "great, democratic maturity" of the Italians, and the State born out of Resistance. Without wishing to detract from the progressive and positive values of our Constitution, it must be said that an entire generation has failed to identify itself with that national pact either because they were the fruit of a previous generation or because they demanded a better one, or simply because it didn't allow them the real space to participate in democracy. The new Red Brigades want to strike out for a re-definition of the rules of the democratic game, on the principle that the worse things are, the better they are. This could be a first watershed in which all of the dissociated terrorists, myself included, could find a tenable position: to support the reforms. But it is a question of "being there" in a relevant sense, as it were making one's own contribution of experience on behalf of that generation which hadn't identified itself in those rules. I envisage my adhesion to democracy as a true adhesion, recognition of the implausibility and of the poisonous nature of armed conflict, in an attempt to create spaces for debate which will prevent its reinstatement. My awareness of the human and political errors, of the tragic import of my actions is a sure one, but I wish to believe that we must ascribe a value to the mourning of past and present years, not because history necessarily has to be nourished by the suffering of men but so that suffering already experienced becomes meaningful.

They are talking about a second republic, perhaps the term is not appropriate, but it is certain that the political and social transformations that have taken place in this country over the last 40 years argue for commensurate improvement on an institutional level. There hasn't been a civil war, but there has certainly been a profound demand for popular participation, and we have moreover witnessed movements representing total rejection of the establishment, whose most extreme position was resorting to "armed criticism". I honestly believe that there can be no society without some sector which wishes to place itself outside that society (indeed the capacity to acknowledge this seems to me to be a maturation of a vision of society devoid of easy utopianism) but the passage from this view to the armed opposition is not automatic. In this dialectic game one may take up two completely different positions: one involves the ability to comprehend the dissatisfaction of which it is the expression, perhaps even the will to sacrifice a part of one's own power thereby; the other involves meeting it in a head-on collision, when the National interest, the state of emergency mentality prevails. I mean that the wind of change which first blew in 1968 was not invariably resolved by recourse to arms.

My warmest regards.

Bruno Laronga

Laronga was arrested in May 1980 and sentenced in 1982 to 13 years' imprisonment by the court in Turin. In December 1983, the Court of Assizes condemned him to life imprisonment at the trials of the Front Line and the Communist Revolutionary Committees.

Domenico Magnetta

First Encounter

I first heard of "Mimmo" Magnetta from the mother of one of the right-wing terrorists I had met in London. These were her exact words to me: "You must meet Mimmo, he's a wonderful young man." I went to meet him in Milan and it was a very happy, very spontaneous meeting. We immediately established a very pleasant relationship.

It was Mimmo who enabled the chaplain of Rebibbia Prison to find the group's weapons cache.

In the meetings I had with him, I saw his awareness of the past and his desire to redeem himself. I also met his wife, I have been to dinner at his home in Milan, and each time we meet it is like a meeting between brothers. I felt in communion with him, and also from a religious point of view he has made great progress and is totally transformed. This transformation has not been limited to the period he has spent in detention when his journey of reconciliation began, but has continued to develop afterwards too, as I have seen.

Letter

Milan, 24th February 1986

Dear Carmelo,

I couldn't help staying on at work (in fact I'm writing to you from the shop when I should be at home) so I could answer your last letter (which gave me great pleasure like all your others) in peace and quiet – and there's plenty of that here!

When you get this letter you'll probably say "at last!" And you're right, I'll tell you that for free, but it hasn't been from lack of goodwill; maybe it was because I've had worries or something but even when I wanted to write to you I just couldn't pick up a pen. But today was different, and so here I am.

I want you to know that my thoughts are often with you and my prayers too. And I would sometimes like to be with you too, but, as you know, because I am under house arrest, that isn't possible yet. And judging by the way things are going here (the appeal is being heard: it's all very rushed and they don't care or want to find out if the people they're judging are the "same" as the ones that committed the crimes all those years ago) it could be that the chances of me coming over to see you are even more remote. I've been given eight years and two months in the first instance and there could be an increase in the sentence. Still, come what may, I feel calm. Even if it's a bit of a pain, just when I'd started to enjoy life again.

The tense situation which has developed because of the recent sad and upsetting events will certainly have a negative effect on the judgement (I am talking about my trial). These were events which I had hoped wouldn't happen again, but as I feared, they have.

And who knows how many other terrible things we still have to see? Because yes, in my opinion, other sad events will be repeated in the near future. And all because as long as this system stays the way it is, full of hypocrisy, injustice, and the more people have of all that the more of it they put in, there will always be people who will do these tragic deeds, although they are becoming more and more isolated.

What makes me angry is that if "our past" had happened on the moon, well, then I could understand why these kind of dreadful things keep happening, but we did what we did right here on earth, and the results, the bereavement and the pain, were and still are visible to everybody today, especially today, in us who committed the crimes and in the people who suffered from them. So going back and making the same gestures all over again is a symptom of insanity (political and human) as well as clear provocation. In fact it's the same old question again, "Who is really benefitting from this?" Excuse the outburst, but it's the least you can say when you see this kind of thinking going on. The kind of thinking that says you've got to strike out to show that you're still alive or just for the sake of doing something, which I always rejected when I was actively involved in certain struggles, well you can imagine what I feel about it now that I'm a different person totally.

Well, I think I've polluted your ears enough for today. Anyway, work is calling me.

I guess we'll be in touch again soon. All my love to you, Carmelo, to all those who are close to you, and not.

When you come to Italy, get in touch. Ciao.

Mimmo

Fulvia Miglietta

I first met Fulvia Miglietta in the women's section of Paliano Prison, near Frosinone, together with a group of prisoners which included Adriana Faranda, Emilia Libera and Francesca Privitera. I remember that my encounter with her was much more profound than with any of the others. She began to let me share a little in her life and what was taking place within her. She was experiencing an almost mystical phase involving a total rejection of the past, with a consciousness of the evil she had done and the knowledge that regeneration was possible, even though she was in prison.

She gives the impression of being a very reserved person, living her own spiritual experience of the rediscovery of God, an experience she can only share with those who understand it. She cannot open her heart to everyone because her experience is different from that of her fellow prisoners, with whom she is nonetheless obliged to spend all her time. To outsiders she appears to withdraw inside herself but I have seen her make her first steps along a beautiful and spiritually elevated path.

Letters

Paliano Prison, 27th November 1986

My dear Carmelo,

I received your letter with great joy. Thank you for your friendship which I sincerely reciprocate. Thank you for the lovely reproductions of Kikko's drawings. They're very beautiful and I'm going to make some little frames for them.

Thank you also for relating the experiences of your itinerancy in New York and your pastoral work in prisons: it was a lovely present. Before starting this letter I read

119

them over again with Michela and we were very moved and touched by them, but also entertained, because we'd met you and it was like having you here in front of us. Together with you I praise and thank the Lord for the great gift of conversion which he gave to you after a period of deep rebellion. I too thank him continually, every day, because he took me by the hand at a time of profound despair, a time when suicide seemed the most natural course for me.

I shall never forget that I was living in hell and that he pulled me out when I asked for his help, looking at the Cross on a church tower in the distance while I was in prison in Voghera. But in time and if you want me to, I'll tell you more about the mercy of our Father and about his great love. As I write I find myself smiling because my joy is renewed every time I think about how he has saved me and how tenacious and persevering he has been in his immense love. I will tell you all about it some time. I just didn't want to wait too long before answering your letter.

Thank you too for Kikko's article where he gives a slightly longer introduction to the "neo-catechumenal Way". I believe Rossella is developing her friendship with your friends in Rome. I'll wait to hear from you again because I think that she spent the whole of Sunday 23rd with them. During the time she was here she certainly gave me the impression that she had made some precious discovery and that the whole basis of her life is slowly changing. I thank the Lord for this too. I'm wishing you a happy Christmas a little early because I'm not sure if you're still at the same address. May Christmas bring us much peace!

All my love.

Fulvia

Paliano, Christmas 1986

My dear Carmelo,

It's been quite a while since I last wrote to you. I wonder if you have received my little letters? I've been allowed to go home for Christmas... after so many years... It will be a sweet sensation because I'll be returning home after rediscovering the value of the family and the love that's there. Love gives substance to everything.

Goodbye then, my dear Carmelo, I wish you a happy and holy Christmas.

All my love.

Fulvia

Paliano, 15th March 1987

My dear Carmelo,

I received your enormous card at Christmas with the season's greetings and your words of affection.

Yes, I wish I too could see all our brothers and sisters in the light of that flame of love which unites us in the one true love.

I also know that everything must be the fruit of suffering and patience and by "rending one's heart and not one's garments". We would all love to see you again but some difficulties have arisen: patience. If it is the will of God we will meet, irrespective of human will. Rossella will come and visit me at the end of the month and I'll get her to tell me about your meeting.

Rossella has begun a way of faith which is vital and as fresh as a spring of water, thanks also to her meeting you and your friends of the neo-catechumenate in Rome. Dear Carmelo, I wish you an Easter full of the happiness of the Risen One who is our joy.

I send you all my love and best wishes.

Fulvia

Paliano, 14th May 1987

My dear Carmelo,

I was very happy to receive your Easter greetings as well as the magazine of the Italian community in London and the lovely photos of the two weddings. What strikes me is your constant smile and I hope that one day, little by little, I will be able to smile too, since I am sure that there are more things to be happy about than sad.

I would so much like to see you and to continue our

dialogue where we left off. Of course I will pray to the Lord to give you the heart for conversion and you must pray to him to give me a heart full of mercy. I often feel hard and demanding towards my brothers and sisters, above all towards those most in need, those who are far away.

The schooling which the Lord is giving me here in prison to bend my selfish will is tough and I would like to tell you about it. I hope that the opportunity will arise. Adriana and Emilia were overjoyed to receive your greetings. Apart from them there's still Giovanna and Francesca here. Michela, Isabella and Assunta are out. Assunta will soon be back. What a wonderful Easter night you had, radiant with joy! Yes, it would really be wonderful to take part in such a celebration.

Rossella continues on her path to conversion and she's happy.

Dear Carmelo, thankyou for remembering us and don't forget I am counting on your prayers to help change my heart. I send you my fondest regards.

Fulvia

Paliano, 25th October 1987

My dear Carmelo,

The letter you wrote telling me a bit about the various stages of your marvellous and hectic trip arrived some time ago. I'm really looking forward to seeing you and hearing about it. Recently I had permission to go home and while I was there I met a dear friend who is suffering because of her son who is under arrest. She said she was going to talk to you about him, having heard about your willingness to reach those who are most alone, wherever they may be. You know the loneliness one experiences in prison. Well, whenever I was going through a time of particular suffering the Lord always provided a friend, whether religious or not, to give the necessary word of encouragement.

A few days ago they took me to ... prison to act as witness in a trial which, thank God, ended favourably for the defendant. While I was staying in this prison, which is the subject of an inquiry by the Ministry of Justice because it's the worst in Italy, I went through the experience of the violence and awfulness of those places all over again: weird insects everywhere, lights on all night, a ghastly relationship with the people who are obliged to work in such a degrading environment. During this time I prayed continuously to have that peace which only the Lord can give, even though I was in that place. And as I prayed one thing became clear: that it's not people who are wicked, it is evil itself which, in certain places where there is no love, takes complete control. But to pray for your enemies, to feel they are your brothers and sisters even though they are forcing other people to live in those appalling conditions, is something which, although I managed it, made me feel ill and caused me a fair bit of confusion.

When I see bullying and persecution it's still difficult for me not to see the people who are committing these acts too. I know very well that each one of them has been saved by Jesus just like me and I also know that they are not really aware of the harm they are doing, just as I wasn't really aware of it when I was hurting others. The problem is that when I talk about the harm that's done to all the people who end up in these places, I feel as though I'm adding my own piece of rancour and resentment to the great mosaic of hate and division which exists between human beings. But on the other hand I'm not prepared to keep silent about it or to lay the blame on an abstraction. I am sure that your own personal experience has made you reflect at length on situations as bad and probably worse than these, and I'd like to hear your thoughts on the subject to know how you have confronted the problem of injustice. If you have time, read the account of my experiences which I wrote for a friend, where I talk about the prison in which I was kept locked up 23 hours a day.

That was in '83 and things were already pretty bad but now they've got even worse. Last year a friend of mine wrote to me from prison telling me about the oppressive and degrading conditions she was living in (infested by rats, bedbugs and fleas, disgusting food and the fear of picking up contagious diseases). When this letter arrived

I sent it, together with some of my own thoughts on the absence of love, to a person who comes to visit us here. It seemed right to me to stand up for other people who end up in such totally appalling situations. But when it's me suffering, and I accept it, saying that the Lord will transform this sea of evil into good, why then do I feel so confused and illogical when I speak out against it? God knows if I've managed to make myself clear. Anyway, the point is that if someone points out an injustice to me I do what I can, within the narrow limits of what is possible for me; but if it is me suffering the injustice, I feel I should bear with it and try not to talk about it so as not to fan the flames of hatred which are already blazing. Can you understand what I'm saying? I hope you'll answer me soon.

I'm sending you best wishes and greetings on behalf of the other girls as well. Much love.

Fulvia

Paliano, 7th November 1987

My dear Carmelo,

I have just received your letter of 29th October. I hope that in the meantime you have received the one I wrote on 25th October. I think the idea of publishing the letters you have been sent is a very good one because they are a sign of the hope which can be born even in places of profound suffering and desperation. I state once more that our God is always close to each one of us, even when we suffer total despair and the contempt of men. But I do hope it won't make it seem as if it's prison which leads people to meet God, because God is a father and he suffers greatly on account of our personal sufferings. Prisons are a cause of deep suffering for him as they are for us. One hopes that men can grow in love and so too in their capacity for forgiveness and helping others, rather than in repression and seeking revenge. Recently I wrote a long letter to Dr Amato, the Director-General of Penal Institutions, giving vent to my feelings about the suffering caused by prisons. I'll let you know what happens. All my love.

Fulvia

P.S. Thanks for the lovely photographs of your trip. Why don't you come and tell us about it? Everyone sends their love. Emilia enjoyed your letter very much and keeps on saying that she has to answer it. Ciao.

Paliano, 2nd March 1988

My dear Carmelo,

I'm answering your letter of 22nd February 1988. I'm continuing on my way to conversion, and it reveals something new to me every day, both about my past and about how to live in the present. I'm sure that you have had letters which bear witness to the various stages along this way.

Goodbye Carmelo, and I wish you success in your work especially in the delicate area of prison life where loneliness is great and where often, sadly, all hope is extinguished. All my love.

Fulvia

Paliano, 10th April 1988

My dear Carmelo,

Coming back here after spending some time at home, I found your letter and I'm answering it straight away. As I told you, my path of conversion is sometimes marked by moments of anguish. For instance, just after the Christmas festivities which I spent outside prison, in freedom, and with the people I love, I couldn't bear the idea of living through all this. It seemed impossible to live with love in this situation and I was greatly tempted to close myself up in my own selfishness, something you often do in prison.

But that meant going into that tunnel of maladjustment which it's so difficult to get out of. I prayed a great deal at that time and it became clear to me that I was unable to accept my suffering because the Lord was not absolute in my life. I was helped by some cassettes given to me by a friend who is a Revivalist priest: they were about the necessity of living without attachments of any sort. Of course it's impossible, but when Jesus is first in your life, then the whole Gospel becomes possible. Some friends of mine in a Baptist community in Rome sent me some tapes too, just to reinforce everything I was going through in that period. They helped me too, with their prayers as well as the religious material that they sent me.

The marvels of God truly never cease to amaze. I find myself here, excluded from the riches community life has to offer, far away from any concrete form of religion, and yet the Lord, through my friends, makes it possible for me to experience his pedagogy. It's wonderful, isn't it?

Ciao Carmelo; I send you all my love, and thanks for your good wishes which I reciprocate.

Fulvia

Paliano, 11th October 1988

My dear Carmelo,

I've been meaning to write for a while and to thank you for your letter of 5th September. You're right about Marco. Like you, I hope in the peace and joy of the Lord, that he's free at last from all wretched human judgements. I'm sorry we won't see each other when you come round the Italian prisons.

This year I met a really "special" person. He lives in the Bronx now, with his wife and seven children. He was here from May until August or the beginning of September to teach us how to programme with computers. The course was organised by the Lazio regional authorities. I followed it every day and even though I found it an effort it got me out of my usual boring routine. But what encouraged me more was the personality of our teacher: seeing him so ready to help, so attentive to everyone's needs and so full of love was a very powerful sign for me. He did more than just teach us; he "gave" his knowledge, like a gift, without reserve. It was his presence which led me to reflect upon my indifference towards the people whom the will of God has brought me to live with today. It enabled me to discover that I am a very proud and egocentric person. It was very salutary to recognize this root of sin because at last the Lord has taken the first place in my heart instead of my ego. Of course it's difficult to get out of that mess of wickedness inside me. But thanks to the presence of God the impossible is now becoming possible. I am very glad about this conversion which is continuing even if some days I feel really depressed. I promised ... that I would write to a priest friend of his to tell him about this incredible and marvellous opportunity for change which God has given me. But I haven't got round to it yet.

As I was saying, I completed the course but I just couldn't make head or tail of computing. You can't imagine how frustrated I felt! I persevered though because I understood even this was one of God's gifts. At the end there was an exam, which everyone passed. I didn't take it because, as I said, I hadn't understood a thing. I only started to make some sense of it towards the end of the course.

Dear Carmelo, thank-you for the photos which you sent with the previous letter and thank you for your friendship.

All my love and affection to you.

Fulvia

Fulvia Miglietta, 47, was arrested in 1981. Sentenced in 1982 for crimes committed whilst a member of the Red Brigades, she dissociated herself from the armed struggle in January 1983. Shortly afterwards she revealed the location of the secret passage near Ventimiglia which was used by the Red Brigades to reach France and for smuggling arms and explosives.

Silveria Russo

First Encounter

I first met Silveria Russo a few years ago in Bergamo Prison, together with Ettorina Zaccheo. She was already married to Bruno Laronga. Right from the start, we established a very pleasant and cordial relationship: she began talking about her past experiences and the world of prison, proposing solutions for the future – not only political solutions for the good of society, but also personal solutions for her own family life.

In her I witnessed a terrorist change roles and become a mother, attain maturity, and enter into a new phase of her life. She spoke to me more than any of the others about the future, about how to reintegrate herself into society – not by washing her hands of her past, but by thinking how to rebuild her own life and the lives of others, in an active and energetic way.

Letters

Bergamo, 22nd November 1986

My dear Carmelo,

I'm writing to you in my terrible handwriting (that's what everyone else thinks) because typing wears me out after a while. Tell me if you can't read it.

I'm sorry if I haven't written to you sooner, but I spend the whole day working and studying without a moment's break. Of course my letter-writing is what gets neglected, but in any case I feel less and less like communicating that way. I really wish these conversations could be face-to-face, because it's so important to be able to hear the person you're talking to. Still, I'm sure that we'll find a better way of keeping in touch, as soon as we start living amongst other people again, and especially our friends.

128

There's no particular news here, the atmosphere's fairly stagnant and each of us is trying to find his or her own way of gradually getting back into normal life. So it's a waiting phase, you see, but there's also a strong feeling of hope.

When are you coming to see us again? If we don't see each other before then, have a happy Christmas.

Lots of love.

Silveria

Milan, 6th February 1988.

My dear Carmelo,

When I tried to tell you about my experiences as an ex-terrorist, I had two problems: on the one hand, I had to explain it all to you objectively and realistically, so it would be comprehensible too, without trying to glamourize a story full of dramatic events and real pain; and on the other hand I had to find a way of getting across that tiny element of valid human experience which the writer was still able to gain from it all.

I mean that it would be easier for me to tell the story of myself as I used to be, and so perhaps try to absolve myself of guilt, and then I wouldn't have to privately admit failure, and admit wasting fifteen years of my life for no reason. I think it would have been an easier option, as if I was learning now for the first time what my experiences had actually been.

But all the people from that past, myself included, return to live amongst us; they're real men and women who've thought about their guilt and have sometimes touched the very bottom, people who have lost themselves and their own identity and their own roots in the human and moral desolation which they themselves have created – these people now find to some extent that they can return to the same society they once fought against, delirious with their own power, and now they have to come to terms with re-integrating themselves into it, and it's neither easy nor painless, because it's still not clear what kind of reaction public opinion will have to their presence. That's today's story, and that's the one which I want to tell now.

My own personal experience is the same as that of many young people who were politically active in and around 1968: there was the movement, the search for a better kind of life (and for many of us women, this became a feminist issue), and making more and more radical decisions until we reached the conclusion that nothing could be changed without recourse to arms. So in '74 and '75, having decided to abandon operating in groups because it was getting us nowhere, we chose armed combat.

At first, it was a choice we made within the movement, but then, as the movement gradually became a less and less concrete reality, and less and less related to a specific group of people, it became a struggle for survival that was totally unrelated to reason, an exercise of violence beyond every human limit. It was a perverse game which destroyed innocent lives because they'd been reduced to the level of symbols, and crushed our own existences because we'd reduced ourselves to the level of fighting machines; a delirium from which we were violently extracted only by the harsh reality of imprisonment from 1980 onwards.

First we suffered the undoing of a network of relationships; the loss of identity; all our convictions were in crisis, then our whole way of thinking of ourselves as important players in a worldwide drama. This was the natural result of the whole process of reflection we went through, but it was above all a problem which went beyond the actual experience we'd been through and led us to think deeply about the whole business of political and social activity, and about the usefulness of our own testimony. Our experience during these few years was made up of questions like these, and it was during this time that we made our decisions both as individuals and as a group.

As a result of these reflections, at last, and in the consciousness of the evil we had inflicted and how profoundly responsible we were for what had happened, we were able to make our first group decision: the decision to renounce our beliefs. Then, gradually, we progressed to a more and more heartfelt admission of our responsibility, knowing as we did that there could be no possible excuses to justify our past acts of violence, but rather the necessity of placing ourselves in full view, not shielded in any way, in order to become human beings once again.

Then the United Groups were formed by right and left-wing ex-terrorists as a common area for discussion, and they helped to turn prison into somewhere where progress and communication could happen – all these stages on our route back to normal life are pretty well known now – until at last certain legal reforms (the Law of Renunciation and the Gozzini Law, which permits shortening of sentences for terrorists who renounce the principle of armed struggle and collaborate with the judiciary, and which is not concerned solely with political crimes, but has opened up the way to an entirely new conception of punishment), enabled us to make this real, concrete and tangible return to normal life; it was a testing process for our new resolutions as well as a model for our re-integration into society.

But during our years of reflection and later, as we made our choice of renunciation explicit, each of us followed his own route; every one of us trod the same pathways as the others but in entirely individual ways which cannot be compared with anyone else's. This is the great strength which lies within the process of becoming whole again, and is to my mind our most important achievement too, because it guarantees that each individual's process of self-criticism is not a short-cut, an easy way out, but a profound and personal transformation of his own conscience.

In fact, I reckon it would be disastrous if it were otherwise, if this extra dimension of individual progress were to be revoked once again by forces greater than the individual, his needs and feelings: we would all return to our former negative state of mind where all cynicism and all destruction of everything human are justified. It's a state which I personally can see cropping up again in our relationship with society, which still presents itself as an exchange of self-appointed guardians of the common good.

I believe, therefore, that the process of renunciation which takes place during this period is sincere and valid in proportion as the subject is able to make the choice himself, and depends on him being able to return to humanity and to the basic values of humanity, and rise up again, and find the strength to approach the rest of the human race once again.

So we set off again, with this collective and agonizing conscience of the wrong we have done, with the humility of pilgrims who return among their own people and ask for their help, even though they have only their newfound wisdom to offer in return, the story of how a man changed, to anyone who wants to listen to it.

And that's the way things are now. There's no longer a category or set of categories which can be identified by some legal formula, just single men and women who want to and can return to life, people who know and can tell you that it's a downward path too, and one which never has a guaranteed destination. In the first place, there's the risk of finding oneself alone in the search for a new identity, or vice versa; to be set up as a figure from the past for reasons which have nothing to do with one's own personal needs. That's a price which it's partly necessary to pay; but for how long, I ask myself, must we remain in the public mind as vague figures who merely stand for the people we really are?

I rather think that if this society really means to give back to democracy some of the energy that has been dispersed, then concrete solutions have to be devised. Solutions which respect all parties and allow those people who acted and suffered during those tragic years to be heard again, and their demands to be listened to, avoiding any taint of the barter mentality.

So help us, all of you, not to be forever handicapped, forever marked by what happened. We ask you this in the same spirit that we asked you before to help us see our mistakes. We can only climb up out of this chasm by becoming responsible adults once again, called upon to contribute actively to the renewal and strengthening of our society, with all the human spirit which comes from our new wisdom, but also with our desire to bear witness to what has been done.

Many of us, in these last few years, have rediscovered our lost faith and so have given a new meaning to our lives. It's like setting off again on a journey that has been interrupted, finding a lost set of values, wanting to express oneself again.

I believe that having a family, children, wanting to discover new things together with others, is the simplest, yet the truest desire that is capable of motivating us.

Coming back to myself, at the end of the terrorist experience, I've found a deep need/desire for love, sharing – old feelings rediscovered in a new form. The search for social solidarity, for example, is one which still fascinates me, but I want it to be a comprehensible, day-to-day solidarity. Having a son, setting up my family again – it's been a tangible, transformative choice for me to make, my turning-point, the point where I've started anew. There's still a whole world waiting to be rebuilt; hopes are high; let's hope we're not going to be disappointed.

Much love.

Silveria

Silveria Russo was born in Bologna on 29th May 1950. She was held from 1980 for various acts of terrorism committed as member and organiser of an armed group called Prima Linea (The Front Line): homicide, kidnapping, assault, etc. Since 1983 she has disassociated herself from them, and helped in 1985 to form, with others, the United Group within Bergamo jail; having been awarded parole for good conduct in early 1987, she served a suspended sentence whilst pregnant, and returned to Milan, where her son Gabriele was later born. She has been married since 1982 to Bruno Laronga, another terrorist from the Prima Linea. Their marriage was subsequently blessed in jail, at San Vittore, in 1984. She is currently condemned to 30 years' imprisonment, but the sentence has been reduced by a half under the Law of Dissociation. She is awaiting appeal procedures regarding the specific criminal acts for which she was jailed in the first instance. Gabriele was born in April 1988.

Isabella Vetrani

Letters

Rome, 25th March 1987

Dearest Carmelo,

"The peace of the Lord be with you." After a long silence on your part, I decided to write and get some news of you. Where have you been? We've asked nearly everyone so as to find out if you'd been in touch with them at least. But they don't know either, so here I am with pen in hand hoping at last to get some news of you.

Here thank God everything is all right. Paolo is carrying on with his job in spite of some difficulties. Actually I should explain that he formed a partnership with a friend from his past (I don't have to tell you how) because we had more than a few financial problems. But it appears that all this wasn't in God's plans, whose wish it was that their company should fail. I can assure you, Carmelo, that this made me very happy because if some people want to have done away with a chapter in their life then they must have done away with certain people as well. Because one way or another those people are always going to get you mixed up in some shady business, that's why I never tire of thanking Him because I see that God had our best interests at heart and most of all wants us to be different from before. Now, in spite of some difficulties, we're on our way up again but none of that frightens us, in fact, conscious of the presence of God, we feel much stronger than before.

I'm doing the second scrutiny of the Neo-catechumenal Way, you can appreciate how I feel. I really feel that God is working inside me and all this makes me very happy because I finally feel loved by Him and, despite the revolution that He's creating inside me, I feel marvellously calm. Believe me, Carmelo, it's something bigger than me because discovering some of the things I have about myself would have thrown me into total despair and that hasn't happened at all. That's why I never tire of blessing God.

I often look back on my past and I feel a great sense of shame for what I was, for all the things that I did. You can't imagine what I feel and I think all the time that it would have been better if I had met God before. Because even though I've only been in the Neo-catechumenal Way for ten years, I've only felt for a short time that He is the Lord of my life. Anyway, if all this was necessary for my conversion, I thank God that all this has happened, otherwise perhaps today I wouldn't be able to appreciate all this.

You know, my Community is giving a catechesis at the Parish of the Canadian Martyrs here in Rome. Just think: such a young community called to such a great task; till now about 150 people have been coming to listen. I hope that they will all stay; but, obviously, it will be God who decides. Paolo has returned to the Way after a long period of absence; see how the Lord is working with us?

Well, I hope to hear from you soon. Remember us always in your prayers, as you are always in ours.

A warm embrace from all of us.

Isabella, Paolo and all the children

Rome, 3rd April 1988

Dearest Carmelo,

Here I am again, after a long gap. But I'm always happy to spend time with you, even if it's only in a letter, to tell you about us, about my life since I started out on my path to conversion and before then too, that is, I mean when the Lord hadn't touched my heart yet.

My past history, as you know, is linked to Paolo's, but it's also linked to the right-wing organizations which I was active in. I've only realized now that I had joined them because I wanted to come out politically at all costs. First I joined the Italian Social Movement, the extreme right-wing party, and became secretary to the "National Volunteers" group. At first I'd done it to help the people who'd strayed from the party, people who were in prison; all the stragglers, without realising that I was just being exploited by other people.

In 1975 I met Paolo. I was proud of being the only woman who was anyone in the extreme right. Then when Paolo went on the run I went with him, living a strange existence, outside this world completely. When you're on the run you don't have a real existence anymore, doing things doesn't bother you any more. You experience the ultimate in dishumanity, as long as you're saving your own skin you wouldn't stop at killing everyone else.

It was an experience that I've never forgotten since, not even when I started the Way in the communities. A feeling of hanging in emptiness, of living a life which isn't true, which isn't life at all.

Just like I haven't forgotten how I felt when I went to see Paolo in prison, after he'd been on a long hunger strike (his weight was down to just 6 stone!) and he was admitted to the criminal psychiatric hospital at Montelupo Fiorentino, because he'd refused every kind of therapy they'd tried. When I saw him there, nearly at death's door, I had this feeling of nothingness, this feeling of a wall in front of me. Then I decided to act, to get him out of there. But there was very little that was humanly possible. Anyway, his release from prison had been stopped by the escape of Scalzone from France.

One evening in the community I told the brothers of my trouble. One of them asked everybody to say the Lord's Prayer for Paolo, since nothing else was humanly possible to help him. "I shall pull you out from the pit of death" the brothers prayed. And the Lord pulled me out of that pit. Paolo lived and returned to us.

I lived through the hardest experiences, as a fugitive, a bandit's woman, spurned by everyone. On many occasions, God has helped me by not letting weapons into my hand, or I would have used them. Now I can't stand the sight of guns, not even toy ones. My children have never played with them either. Some time ago a friend of mine asked me: "How come you decided not to come out politically even when you'd got to the top?" "I didn't start coming out – I answered him – but I began to live when I said yes to the Lord. I said no to death and yes to life".

Now that Paolo is here and working for us, it feels like a dream, after all those years of hardship and suffering.

Some time ago the parish priest of San Giuseppe, my parish, who had always helped me in those difficult times, offered me some money to help us. I refused, and explained that we were coping now. He was amazed. "You could have taken it anyway – he said – people never say no to money." And he added: "You know, Isabella, no one would have bothered to bet a false penny on you people, but you are showing them that there's hope in the world, because no one would have believed you could lead honest and normal lives".

Carmelo, I'm not telling you this to reflect glory on me but on God. May the Lord grant you his peace.

Isabella

Ettorina Zaccheo

First encounter

In my opinion, Ettorina is a deeply spiritual person, who is fully aware of her wrongdoing and the necessity of paying the price. The bloody and anguished experiences of her past are a burden but she does not try to forget, because she cannot forget. She replied to my message of hope and faith by saying: "No, we cannot allow ourselves to forget. I must pay".

I have never found such a strong feeling of needing to pay for wrongdoing in any other person. All the others were obviously happy to leave prison, it is what they desire most, but in her this desire to pay prevails.

The last meeting I had with Ettorina was probably one of the most moving I have ever had with an ex-terrorist. We talked for about an hour and a half. She wept uncontrollably at my words of courage and sympathy.

During another meeting, I don't remember if it was the first, she told me of the anguish she felt at the presence of the wife of one of her victims who sat in front of her for the entire duration of the trial. She told me, "I couldn't bear the sight of her any longer, it was a constant condemnation to see that person in front of me who seemed to accuse me just with her presence". I believe that this was one of the first things that made her rethink her whole life and expiate her sins.

Letters

Bergamo, 8th December 1986

Dear Father Carmelo,

I too remember meeting you here in Bergamo with happiness; your letter and all the things you sent me arrived at a time when I was making new decisions and looking to the future; it was a time when I was asking myself what I would do with my life when I got out of here. It's not so simple, everyone tends to want to go home, and I want to as well, but it's not that straightforward. It is true that we need to rebuild our lives, and it's true that when we abandoned everything to join the armed struggle, we were motivated by certain things which in my present re-analysis seem more profound than the ideology and group involvement, which now no longer exist. But that first rejection of the past raises questions about the future, I don't know if I will be able or willing to "retire into private life" or else if I will end up involved in some cause again, certainly not in politics, I don't want to hear another word about that, but perhaps working close to poor people, to those who are most in need. You know that I used to be a nurse, I worked in a hospital, and even though my head was stuffed full of Marxist ideology, I know that I was happy in those wards, I stayed on longer than I needed to every day and dedicated all my energy and ability to it. Then I got involved with the unions, the Communist party, and the armed struggle.

Apart from your letter this week, I got one from two friends of mine as well, one of them wrote to me from Africa where he's been working as a missionary for the past two months. He is a non-believer, a layman, but he's decided to stay there for two years. The other is a doctor from Brianza, near Milan, and he's throwing everything up too and going to the Amazon to look after lepers, he's a be-liever and he's leaving on this mission any day now, he's hoping to be there by Christmas. So there are two different people looking for a meaning in life, to giving where it is most needed.

Then I thought about your work, that's a mission too, so you see why I'm asking myself these questions. With all the wrong we have done, perhaps we should do everything in our power to get involved in doing some good.

Right now, after all the experiences I've been through, I'm unlikely to do anything just for emotional reasons or out of a momentary enthusiasm. I'm thinking about all this

139

carefully and I don't believe that these letters I've been getting are a coincidence, they're a sign to help me understand what I want do with myself and with my life. Obviously we can do a great deal in our small way too, but it's a good thing not to get too mellow about it.

I can't tell you about my past in a letter, if we see each other I'll tell you more; I have just been through the Supreme Court of Appeal which has ordered a review of the appeal trial. My sentence was considered excessive – 40 years; it will be reviewed with the new judgement.

Then if the Law of Dissociation is passed, everything will be reviewed a second time; in a year I can hope for some leave and then work outside, some kind of social assistance I hope.

I study and work, even if I am a bit tired of prison group dynamics, especially between us political detainees which you know all about too.

I'm continuing along the path of faith and this gives me great comfort and helps me in my uncertainty.

Thinking of all you're doing in the English prisons helps me to cope with my own situation here, even if I have moments when I get tired of it, but I get over it by thinking of people worse off than me, and people who dedicate themselves to this vital work.

I'll finish this letter by wishing you a happy Christmas, in this time of waiting and prayer. I will remember you, but you pray for me too, we will be close in prayer. Goodbye for now. With much affection.

Rina

Bergamo, 30th July 1988

Dear Father Carmelo,

I was very pleased with the last meeting, I took the exam and it went really well. I told you that I find it difficult right now thinking about the past, the good and the bad times, partly because of the negative aspects of the whole experience and partly because of getting over it, and in this sense, as you know, I'm happier recalling all the various episodes on a personal basis rather than in socio-political terms, or in terms of my attachment at that time to that perverted experience and the process of reconstruction today of what was torn to shreds within me as a total reversal of my whole way of thinking and being, and the search for a peace still not found and yet so necessary. Of course a far greater forgiveness is offered to us every day, but the continual confrontation with other people, the people that we have offended, the people who are near to us, and those in prison who are working towards rehabilitation, that is the benchmark for verifying this change in us all.

We still have a long way to go, fortunately not on our own: there is still so much to learn from the people nearest to us, who have made peace and reconciliation between men a fundamental part of their existence. I believe deeply in this and gain much strength from the continuous confrontation with situations operating in this way, and, as I was telling you, there are little initiatives, little gestures, a sense of giving that may be the key to positively overcoming this whole business.

As far as I am concerned, I can see areas of progress to be made within myself, but I still feel so oppressed; the difference between me and the others is probably just that: some have progressed further in turning this process into a reality, by rebuilding a family, with the joy of children or by a working situation involvement with helping others or by any number of other ways that present themselves. But for the present I am still in prison, with all the impediments and suffering that this implies, even though I am trying to confront it in the most constructive way possible both for myself and for the people around me; it's obvious how much it's wearing me down.

We have squandered a treasure; how can we get it back within ourselves first and foremost, as the possession of peace, of willingness to help others, since alone we are worth so little? It is difficult to overcome egoism and to behave coherently with what we have been lucky enough to rediscover.

Dear Carmelo, as you can see I am in the throes of a painful search for truth and I hope it will provide new opportunities and possibilities... Thinking back to certain episodes from the past still fills me with great pain and future prospects are not yet clear...

Don't think that I am disheartened, despite all this, quite the contrary; all my past experiences have made me believe deeply in what you said; that it's in the very darkest moments that new glimmers of hope appear.

And it is equally certain that God does not abandon us in these moments, so you will see when we meet again that other things will have happened to me along this mountain road which is so steep, but which leads to the summit, where the horizon is so much wider.

I send you my warmest regards; if you have time please write to me.

Ettorina

Ettorina Zaccheo, 34 years old, was sentenced to life imprisonment for membership of an armed band (the Milanese cells of the Red Brigade division known as "Walter Alasia") in December 1984. She renounced her association in July 1985. She was considered head of the "Brigata Ospedaliera Fabrizio Pelli" under the battle name of Sandra.

As a sign of her renunciation she made a full admission of her responsibilities in the armed struggle, without informing on her companions. According to the lawyers, she took responsibility for episodes which were never credited to her. In July 1985 the Milan Court of Assizes sentenced her to 30 years' imprisonment. On 15th May 1986 she signed a document along with 30 or so other ex-Red Brigade members, declaring their renunciation of the principle of armed struggle.

It was the first time that Red Brigade hardliners had become associated with an initiative of this kind. "Our break with the armed struggle", observed the signatories of the document, "is more profound than is apparent from the outside and is so complex that it often results in our total silence. This is interpreted in totally the wrong way, namely, as a sign of a yet more unyielding adherence to our earlier convictions. Undoubtedly the military defeat took its toll, but no defeat in itself necessarily brings about a change in the opinion of the defeated. In our case, however, it has given us occasion to reflect, and this has been decisive. Our motivation, the social reasons which had inspired us since the early 70's, had dried up in us, and doubts and crises of confidence began to arise in us".

The document ends by reminding people of "the capacity of man to change" and asking that thought be given to some sort of "useful social service as a possible alternative to imprisonment".

Arrigo Cavallina's testimony

Letters

Rebibbia, October 1987

Dear Carmelo,

I'm going to tell you the story of my life so that you'll know a bit about my past, as well as seeing me in the present. I taught literature in secondary schools and was an active member of Autonomia Operaria – the Workers Autonomy group – I have been in prison from March '75 until December '77, from June to July '79, from December '79 until today, still no definitive sentence despite the 10 years already served. I was sentenced by the court to 14 years in the trial of the Roman splinter group, the "7th of April Movement" (most serious crime: membership of an armed gang) and to 25 years on appeal in the Milan trial of the "Armed Proletariat for Communism" – (most serious crime: conspiracy to commit murder).

I have written two books and contributed to various newspapers and magazines.

As an inmate in Rebibbia prison I was one of the founders of the so-called "United Group". I am studying for a second degree in law.

Born: 1945. The perfect family environment, full of love, freedom, and no secrets. My parents had a patisserie and coffee shop on the promenade in the centre of Verona. My father was also a violin teacher and leader of the Arena orchestra, sometimes away on tour, and he used to come back home with loads of presents. Musical tradition in family: my grandfather a flautist, my father a violinist, me with a little promise on the piano, quickly abandoned due to complete absence of vocation. Family friends gathered in the evenings to play and listen to quartets (my uncle, second violin). A lay, anti-fascist environment.

143

I was ten when my father died of cancer. I went through a difficult phase of painful shyness and indolence at school, but I think this had more to do with growing up than with my father's passing away. The absence of a paternal figure affected me in other ways: I created models of behaviour for myself which involved adhering to rules of an almost mathematical strictness in my daily life, and an inflexible sense of having to stick to major decisions with unyielding rigidity. I was to witness the consequences of this when the obligations imposed by an erroneous model of behaviour silenced all the natural voices which cried out in horror from within me.

My mother ran the shop alone as long as she could and then she sold it. We lived on the proceeds until I got my accountancy diploma and got my first pay packet working in the Town Hall. My last years at secondary school marked my baptism into political commitment. It involved a cultural quest of such ferocity I fear it must be irrepeatable: literature mostly, then a mixture of other subjects which I can no longer recall: soon after being a superficial Catholic I became a Catholic activist in the parish and soon after that a dissenter, then I considered myself Protestant and even Buddhist for a while (one meeting and a few letters) and finally atheist. A volcanic eruption of new departures marked my student days.

But in the one and only year I belonged to Catholic Action, one afternoon, my heart pounding, slinking along the wall for fear of being recognized, I slipped in the door of the Communist party headquarters and joined the Federation of Young Italian Communists. Today it must seem an insignificant act; at that time, in Verona, and with my background, it was more shocking than streaking along the Via Mazzini.

Why did I do it? I had never even met a factory worker and I didn't express my economic difficulties in anger against society. Hard as I try I can only think of a few books like Cafiero's "Selections from Das Kapital" and Pessenti's "Manual of Political Economy" and perhaps one or two others which I found simply convincing. But if what they spoke of, the exploitation, the class divisions and the inexorable course of history was true, then I was duty-bound to declare my allegiances. To that one party.

I was rapidly disillusioned, the canvassing for membership, the suffocating conformism, their symbol: the desk. I don't know how long it lasted but I soon began to receive Trotskyist and pro-Chinese literature, a pro-Chinese group had been formed in Verona out of the Vietnam committee and suddenly, amidst the prospectless greyness, there was the colour, the sound, the palpable shape of the Revolution; all we had to do was build the new party, bit by bit, since its function had already been engraved in history. Here, at last, was something coherent.

But I wonder: did I know the human tragedy of the Revolution? I don't mean I should have given up, since it was still arguably less worse than the day-to-day scandal of under-development; but I wonder in what light we anticipated the consequences, which we could scarcely ignore, of the suffering inflicted upon ourselves, our families and friends, on the "people"? And I can't answer that. There was perhaps a certain grandeur in the victorious "revolutions" viewed with the benefit of hindsight, in their surviving protagonists, combined with our own dutiful adherence to the progress of history, which took away our freedom to realize and to confront the genuine, doubting, anguished part of ourselves; today I'd call it the part of love.

What do I mean by that? I think I've understood the basic falseness of those inclinations: it lay in an insufficient understanding or care about the individual, in allowing categories to prevail; in thinking that a person who is totally defined by a category can really exist – let alone everyone! – a person to whom one can attribute all those things and only those things which pertain to that category. Those convenient classifications which assist in making an approximate evaluation of a particular phenomenon were made to become the key for a series of links, however "dialectic", from the human being to the social conscience, from the social to the economic being. From class to class hatred.

Thus one arrives at drawing the dividing line, friends on this side, enemies on that. And meanwhile the obvious question remains unasked: enemies with respect to what? With respect to some conflicting interest; but what conflicting interest can there be in a world which reduces the individual to nothing? Even the most fanatical person has deep in his subconscious the natural inclination to communicate his own fanaticism to others; and surely, all truly significant interests, life in this world and hope beyond it, demand solidarity.

To me the other person's point of view seemed the perverse dominance of bad faith. Arrigo – with his external regulations, his lack of compassion, since every encounter with another person is nothing more than the unbearable and dispersive reflection of the encounter with a book (that is, another person who is worthy of consideration) – adheres to the scheme which shows him how and where the world is going and prompts the necessary action. He has all the normal experiences, falling in love, having friends, travelling, going on holiday, but always ... on this side of the line.

My dissociation from the armed struggle has also been a strange voyage of getting to know other people. But how easy it is to define new categories. The repentant terrorists, for example. Even in '86 when, after years of being kept apart, the prisoners of the United Group were mixed with other inmates in Rebibbia Prison there were some who preferred to withdraw and shut themselves up within their category of "political" prisoners.

The rejection of violence is an essential and common point of arrival for dissociation. I have at times been surprised by the form which this rejection takes, but which of course I consider a substantial and decisive step forward. There have been many years when we could not be sure of our own safety, and I'm not just talking about police beatings, but of assaults from other prisoners. I don't think anyone who hasn't experienced it can appreciate how awful it feels expecting to be stabbed; your heart exploding inside you when you hear the sound of a scuffle behind you, or your cell door opening suddenly; you daren't close your eyes while you're washing your hair in the shower. You eye up every new arrival wondering if he's been ordered to kill you. These things have happened and worse. Then all this came to an end and we all met together in December '82, we found ourselves looking at each other with an unbelievable sense of relief.

In this reassuring climate it became possible to realize how much violence there still was inside us: only words were allowed in the war game, nonetheless implacable categories among the so-called "components" of the so-called United Group were created. This provided the opportunity to observe that the need for violence is born from unresolved tensions within us and is always seeking an excuse to come out. Once a large group of prisoners were beating up, amongst general approval, a black inmate. One of them said to me, "We're not beating him up because he's black, we're not racist. We're beating him up because he's queer". We look for official justification or justification from within our own group. There are echoes here of "Rollerball". Some people have a licence to kill little birds for pleasure; others, from the outside, project all the evil within and around them onto prisoners and in their eyes no punishment is sufficient. Today you can see an obvious dividing line between rival football fans. There are so many ways of separating off the alien, of justifying the suppression of his every right (rights belong exclusively to one's own category), to do violence to him while ignoring our own conscience and the censure of our peers.

Not everyone came to the conclusion that violence was the logical consequence of the revolutionary option. When I think back to my wasted past I go back way beyond the years of the armed struggle to the times of the meetings, the party headquarters, the cyclostyled literature, the pamphlet distributing campaigns in the areas frequented by the "proletariat", the systematic reading of the complete works of Marx, Lenin, Mao and all their interpreters. These were all tedious, though necessary, steps in building up the organization, and myself into a professional revolutionary, which I have never been. Then, with your heart racing, learning how to prepare a molotov, how to break into a car. We had to know these techniques to get hold of money and arms because the war of the people was inevitable and who would help, organize, arm the people if we didn't get ourselves ready?

And then the rapid spiral into illegality, the categorisation of the others as enemies, the need to plan ahead, to set an example, to advertise one attack with another, on things, on people, killing. One's own group, which to begin with is nothing more than a temporary expedient, becomes a necessary means, so necessary as to become in itself (its growth, its survival) the real end. It's difficult to refute this descent towards the precipice without criticizing the seed which contained it. But, I repeat, not everyone felt obliged to do their time in the organization out of a sense of duty. Some jumped on to the violence bandwagon as a form of justified oppression (I mean justified in their eyes of course, and in the eyes of their companions, since they found a ready made ideology). Some thought they were denying themselves for the sake of realizing history, others thought they were realizing themselves in those events. Today those who say, "We were wrong but we had a good time", certainly aren't referring to the murders but to the robberies, the mass looting of supermarkets; but I feel ill at ease.

It is for this reason that we must push forward in our self-analysis of the terrorist phenomenon. The dissociation from the armed struggle can and must be sufficient for a political and judicial reappraisal, but to assist individuals in their social growth we must dig deep into our own past. I am afraid of the differences which are made to constitute categories, of seeing in others nothing more than what is on the surface. I am afraid of the limited knowledge of oneself and of others which fosters rather than exposes or dissolves the need for violence.

In 1968 I had been working at the Town Hall for four years. I was a few months away from finishing my degree. "I was there too", involved in that little bit of agitation which rubbed off onto Verona from other cities.

In order to get away from the office I spent a year teaching in the Abruzzo National Park, a year of exile; memories of lessons prepared by candlelight, wrapped up in blankets, as the snow fell in piles off the roof and broke the electric cables (putting the lights, the heating and the water pump out of action). But there was also skiing in the afternoons and the sudden arrival of spring in blossom, yelling out loud, a spring of books and reading.

Then four years of teaching in Verona; I shan't dwell on them. I have indicated my involvement with the groups, the first experiences of learning to commit illegal acts. I developed ties with the Workers Power group, and attended the subversive meetings of the workers at the port of Marghera, near Venice, and in Verona I felt excluded from History.

I was transferred to Milan at the end of '73, I taught in Rho and lived in Cinisello. I often met with ex-members of Workers Power, which had now become Workers Autonomy. This was without doubt the worst period in my life.

Cetta (how can I explain who she is? She's not my wife, we're not married, and I don't want to say my girlfriend because there are echoes of possession in that word which are not appropriate and anyway we go back too far to use such expressions – she's just ... Cetta) was supposed to come and live with me after I settled in. But the whole time, more than a year, she couldn't decide and meanwhile I was nothing more than a political puppet, with no friends, going backwards and forwards by car, with my packed lunch and sleep in my eyes, between school and meetings, prepared to risk everything out of a sense of duty and suffocating every voice within me which refused out of fear and probably out of natural good sense. The worst crime took place in March '75: it was a robbery in the apartment of an arms collector. The preparations and the aborted attempts had taken quite a while and I remember how I felt alone amongst the others; tiredness, forebodings, uneasiness. The day after the successful robbery I was arrested. I still had our plans in my pocket, a kind of suicide.

I have written a lot about the three years I spent in prison (I got out in December '77), I gathered together the correspondence and other stuff in two books. Here I just want to point out two things.

One is the fact of being forced to live with others. Even

under normal conditions the lack of a space of one's own, of a little privacy, leads to exasperation. This caused me no little suffering, but at the same time – because I came from the opposite form of exasperation, of loneliness, not in my political activities but in every other human experience – I was more affected by another, stranger experience: the discovery of the other side, the encounter with him. The categories had not yet been abolished, but on this side of the dividing line the prisoners were no longer reduced to mere class brothers (despite my theorising attempts to see them as such), but recognized at last to be three-dimensional people, each one with an irreducible wealth, with a distinctive individuality, an accumulation of affections, of mistakes and pain to which I could not be indifferent. These unusual friendships were consolidated by that other violence, the one that always goes unpunished, the violence not of the institutions as such, but of some of its laws, structures, parts, of certain personnel.

It is necessary to reflect on one serious matter even if it is difficult. I want to make it clear that I am not making allowances for myself. To destroy someone else's life is not only a crime but causes enormous suffering, a responsibility which one can never shed, whatever one's motives may have been. This said, it is still useful to question oneself about motives.

The so-called armed struggle has been defeated because it reflected the ideologies and the distorted aspirations of those who practised it and a few others. The blood has washed away any positive reaction which in the beginning might have been elicited in the public. The ideology had thus to take into account the people's rejection and to balance the few and miserable satisfactions against the risk both of losing one's life and of prison. Inevitably it was a descending curve. I doubt that the betrayals and the subsequent entrenchments were ever a decisive step forward. On the other hand what prolonged terrorism, and I say this because it has been my own experience, was the decision to visit a merciless destruction upon us: laws and emergency legislation extending the length of sentences to kingdom come, the feeling of coming up against a brick wall. And then, once convicted, not the empty passage of time, but the programmatic violence of the Special Prisons.

My first years were a descent into the inhuman until the Special Prison of Novara was opened. My mother and Cetta looked at me through the glass, asking questions, and I with my head on the table straining to hear their voices through the intercom. They had the sensation of something terrible without understanding what it was. The attendant guard was there, ready to draw non-existent conclusions from my replies. We could be beaten every eight hours exactly and hit with batons as we went in and out to the exercise yard, plus all the humiliating rules, "Yes Sir, Good Morning, Sir", standing to attention, moving at the double with your hands behind your back, and this was no free regime of spontaneous brutality. Everything was calculated to the last detail in advance.

By whom and why?

There are a lot of other things about the Special Prisons which are pretty well known now. I was lucky enough to get out but those who have stayed there, turning into lifers, haven't had the opportunity to see the other face of the State. Prison was no longer a "school of revolution" as those who still believed in the revolution had foolishly told themselves, but rather an accumulator of the worst part of us, of desperation, anger, hatred, theories about who the "real men" were.

One thing which all prison inmates agree on is that the worst beatings are the ones the others give you. When you hear the screams from the next cell you're marked forever. It's a matter of instinct. Among terrorist groups there is a mixture of desperation and solidarity, inside and outside prison, a solidarity strengthened in relation to the techniques of punishment. How was it possible that all the scientific knowledge of the punitive state, ranging from prison design to the training of staff, was matched only by an ingenuousness which was incapable of understanding that its actions conspired to prolong or to provide more reasons for terrorism? One wonders which interests, even more criminal than our own, were exploiting the events we

151

were involved in and are still active today, unexposed, behind respectable facades.

I repeat that I am not making allowances for our behaviour. It is simply a refusal to offer ourselves up, condemned and set apart, guilty of all the evil of those years. Symbols of failure and reformation, yes, on condition though that it be realized that the difference between murderers and non-murderers does not lower perimeter walls or reduce sentences.

My mother was worn down by my time in prison. She held out for as long as she could help me; when I came out she fell victim to cancer. '78 and '79 were my last years of freedom, tragic and beautiful. I spent most of the time looking after my mother at home and in hospital. A few months later Cetta's mother died of cancer then a few months later her father.

But I spent part of the time living very intensely for myself: friends, self-analysis, up in the mountains, camping, the flute, and love, at first very hard, full of thorns, and then rebuilt. After all our family sorrows Cetta and I were like two playing cards resting against each other, holding each other up. I remember that I became aware of the "political" notion that freedom is not a shift or an appropriation of power, but the ability to recognize where other people's power deforms you, in your body, in what you buy, in your desires; and to retreat instead, and look for the truth about yourself, about nature and about humanity.

When I look back at the past, amongst my many regrets, I am helped only by the continuity of the sense of solidarity which I felt with those who were still in prison. I was filled with all the anger of a victim who has been spared and I couldn't concern myself with my own happiness without thinking of their suffering. I did many things which were right and probably good. But I also formed that little group of wretches which, while seeking to deal with the "prison issue", contributed its tally of blood to make those years ugly and unbearable. My dissociation is the story of dissociation from the amalgam of solidarity and violence, the incompatibility of which was neither immediately apparent nor quickly grasped.

I think that prison had made me blind. It had at any rate made me unreceptive to the invigorated culture of the new movements, that multitude of reappraisals and new experiences which had grown out of the rejection of all political ideology. As I became interested in it and came to know it I began to criticize my own little armed group. At first, only certain effects of the violence, that vicious circle which contained within itself the impossibility of its own success. In order for an illegal organization to survive and to keep in training it needs dedication; you don't have time for restoring your forces. You think you're fighting for improvements when all the while you're trapped by the values of the instruments you use, which are the oldest ones in the world, and exactly the same as your enemies'. In one sense the gun cannot remain a mere tool, it is you who become an appendage of the gun, which imposes its own laws and its own culture.

Then the consequences: the same acts which perhaps for a while were able to prevent more beatings in a certain place, or to hinder the transformation of a detention centre into a Special Prison, were also responsible for intensifying the climate of hardness. I think that a large part of the emergency legislation was a direct response to this kind of violent struggle against the state of emergency. Then the people: it was only the delirious ravings of journalists which dreamed up the people's concurrence in the struggle. I remember the impression I got from looking at a large beach on the Romagna coast. If this was the "people" in freedom away from work, if this was how it practised the only kind of relationship with nature it could imagine, then ours was a completely lost cause, there was simply nothing to change. A fairly aristocratic sense of total defeat no doubt, for even my "comrades" in their non-politically-active freedom were no different from the "people".

It's clear that this was just another category; if you'd gone to talk to the people under their parasols you'd have found individuals with multifarious facets because of course no-one truly fits the description of a consumer society robot, if only because robots don't suffer...

A feeling of ever-increasing tragedy pervaded me. The

sound of a walkie-talkie, a car door slamming in the night and my heart was in my mouth, they were coming to get me, my life was over. Not only had I given up, I tried to convince others that to carry on taking risks inevitably increased the probability of going over the edge of the precipice. I think that some of the others were aware of this but that absence of any proposal of alternative values made them accept, perhaps even pursue, our total collapse.

There's a question too I don't know whether to answer: why didn't we get any messages? I mean something which didn't contradict any of the things we were looking for deep-down, but suggested some alternative commitments for us to make? Now I know that the door wasn't slammed shut in our face; recently for instance I have read articles written then by Bobbio and Cardinal Martini which are enough to put anyone in a crisis of doubt. Why didn't they reach us? Why didn't we get to know about them? Why didn't they drop on top of us with all the weight of a cultural emergency?

One morning in August '79, on the island of Elba, as I sat on the stony grass overlooking the clear waters and gazing out at the flat outline of Pianosa prison (a premonition perhaps?), I began to do some yoga from a little book I had brought on holiday with me. I liked it and I've carried on doing it to this day. It was my first serene dialogue with my body. Gradually the rhythm of my heartbeat and my breathing became a form of deep communication with the rest of me, a dialogue within myself. This too was a way of discovering a natural ethic which at last was not scientific, nor a model or a duty, just listening faithfully to what we carry inside ourselves.

It was Christmas. Cetta had lost both parents and our love had matured. It looked as if the frustrating game which had always kept us living apart was over and I spent days going round the stalls looking for presents for her. They picked me up while it was still dark on 21st December.

Parma, San Vittore, Regina Coeli, Rebibbia. What many of us felt in these prisons became a much debated issue: dissociation, an idea like a beacon, attractive and persuasive. Yet more extraordinary than the change in us was the change in the prison authorities, who in sharp contrast to their habitual suspiciousness and inertia gradually took some decisive steps, and both recognized our existence and encouraged us.

The dissociation movement is a fragment of public history, perhaps too much so. It's not at all a homogeneous phenomenon, it's like a crowded high street. So often they want to reduce us to a cliché and it's curious how much they distrust dissociation simply because it doesn't conform to their preconceptions.

I can't say whether suffering is useful or not, but when we do suffer it must be part of our growth. Perhaps we would be better people if there weren't any prisons, but we can't know that; what we can know is that not a single instant of our lives is useless: there is no sorrow which can completely take away the meaning of living. This is the deep link between the forgiveness of the victims' families and the remorse of the people in prison who organise their days around building and realizing hope. Amidst the suffering they do not turn in on themselves but become aware of the existence of other values. They are still capable of being happy in the knowledge that no wrong is completely irreparable and that out of the disgust they feel for their past comes a desire to seek a kind of equilibrium and to do something good.

I went through some really bad times before I understood this. Other people were no longer the object of hostility. I passed a rigorous test too: in February '81 I was beaten up by some prison officers and it took me three months in hospital to put me back together, but at no time did I hate them. I refused to be plaintiff for damages in the trial which found them guilty (also out of a desire to be consistent: I ask that my own correspondent state of guilt be healed). My feelings were primarily ones of bewilderment at how they had let themselves negate their humanity to such a degree. Slowly, as the emotions linked to the memories of the evil of the past began to thaw, it was I who became the object of my rancour.

I have received marvellous encouragement from my experiments with yoga and from the witness given by a

Christian whose kindness has been directed simply and affectionately towards me, and not because of anything I might represent. I don't want to talk about discoveries and experiences since I am still caught up in a lot of uncertainty and confusion. I am only the latest person to have set foot upon a very ancient path and I'd have nothing new to say about prayer or the fact that we are not just prisoners for visiting but that we too have the responsibility to give something to those who are worse off than we are, if only because they don't have the gift of the strength to change, to bear with their problems, to wait.

There are, however, wasted opportunities which cry out for redress. When it is recognized that a convict is no longer dangerous he is let out on parole for 45 days a year but then the rest of the time he is forced to suffer as a parasite, useless and separated from the rest of the world. No-one has ever explained to me why this must be our punishment, why the desire to make reparation and our new ethical choices must be rendered fruitless, while on the outside there are endless opportunities, with no threat to other people's jobs, for helping those in need or protecting the nation's heritage, or the environment.

The acceptance of voluntary service as an alternative to detention is the cause to which I am most committed.

And apart from that ... this is Rebibbia Prison, where the officers smile; the same smile which sometimes passes between us, people who are not defined by their role or their uniform. A mass of people, prisoners and non-prisoners, a true cross-section of society, with all its filth, and plenty of opportunities not to waste our time but to make good use of it: getting up early to study, the yoga course, the food science course, editing the prison paper, the co-op producing a film, music, the gardening course, seminars on the 70's, the many friendships which survive and even begin despite the years spent in prison, letters to write, like this one ... and then it's already time for bed.

Yours,

Arrigo

156

Dear Fr Carmelo,

I am sending you a paraphrase of the Miserere that I've written, sorry about the crazy page order.

Affectionately,
Arrigo

Paraphrase of the Miserere [Psalm 51]

God, grant me grace according to your constant tenderness; in the great love of your entrails, in your capacity for putting yourself in my position, wipe out my rebellion against your order. Cleanse me of my disharmony, pull me out of this alternative system that I got lost in. Today you're happy with me, you welcome me just as I am, reveal yourself to me so that I can know you, make me accept others as you accept me, give me the strength and tell me what I can do for their good and change them for the better.

You know, you're watching me to question me, you challenge me and I'm listening to your rebuke. I recognise my blame, my sin is always before me. In what I have done to others and to nature, against you, against you alone have I sinned. In analysing my responsibility I'm not going to get depressed for no reason but I'll carry on my dialogue with you. How was it possible to do something that is evil in your eyes and to your love? But I did it just the same. Every day I wonder what's weighing me down and making me uneasy and how I should have acted differently.

If you were just a judge, I'd have no way out; but you're the injured party and your judgement is forgiveness. My pain derives from this disparity: how could I have offended someone who continues to give his friendship in answer to mine? And I offend him so often when I neglect my relationship with others. I too, when I feel injured, want to reply with forgiveness and friendship.

Look, I was conceived in sin, my mother conceived me in the sin of the world. But you love the truth even in my dark heart and in its intimacy you teach me wisdom, your order, your warmth, your plan for salvation; you make me

157

find out and spur me on to the truth about what I am.

Purify me and I shall be cleansed, wash me and I shall be whiter than snow. Do not look at my sins, wipe out all my faults.

Make me a pure heart and renew in me a steadfast spirit. Don't turn me away from your presence and don't deprive me of your holy spirit. Let me feel the joy of being loved, welcomed, saved; in prayer, in adoration, in silence and in music, in the dialogue of your Word, in contemplation, in sacrifice, in giving, in renunciation, in my inner voice make the gift of your joy explode within me. Certain of your love and your pardon, I ask you to confirm that I am different from before. And just as you have done with me, I know that you can always correct and convert others. Through pardon, friendship and the witness of joy, make me an instrument of salvation. Give me the will and the ability to rebuke with love and for the good of others. Give me the faith in your strength to create new hearts, let me partake in the generosity of your spirit.

I want to bear witness to your mercy. So as to teach your ways and to make sinners turn to you I want to proclaim the truth of your salvation, make sinners turn to you; I want to incarnate this truth in daily practice, pardoning in my turn, keeping my neighbour company, correcting him with love and humility. In the face of every evil and every threat I implore your mercy, your advice and the strength to dedicate myself to resisting evil. God my salvation, free me from the offences that I have committed and I will extol your justice and sing your praises.

A contrite heart is the sacrifice which pleases you. Don't spurn a dejected and humiliated heart. Make my heart's conversion represent to me a commitment for social reconciliation. Let me carry out, with joy, penances that may be useful not just to me but to the whole of humanity, in whose path to conversion I too am a pilgrim.

Arrigo Cavallina, considered one of the ideologues of the group calling itself "Armed Proletarians for Communism" an organization linked with Autonomia Operaia (Workers' Autonomy), was sentenced to 23 years imprisonment on 28th June 1985 by the second court of Assizes in Milan. At present he is under house arrest.